Unity of the Church
and Human Sexuality

Toward a Faithful
United Methodist Witness
Study Guide

HIGHER EDUCATION & MINISTRY
General Board of Higher Education and Ministry
THE UNITED METHODIST CHURCH

Unity of the Church and Human Sexuality: Toward a Faithful United Methodist Witness, Study Guide

The General Board of Higher Education and Ministry leads and serves The United Methodist Church in the recruitment, preparation, nurture, education, and support of Christian leaders—lay and clergy—for the work of making disciples of Jesus Christ for the transformation of the world. Its vision is that a new generation of Christian leaders will commit boldly to Jesus Christ and be characterized by intellectual excellence, moral integrity, spiritual courage, and holiness of heart and life. The General Board of Higher Education and Ministry of The United Methodist Church serves as an advocate for the intellectual life of the church. The Board's mission embodies the Wesleyan tradition of commitment to the education of laypersons and ordained persons by providing access to higher education for all persons.

Contents

Foreword

This study guide is an invitation into holy conversation. It is also an invitation to think deeply about who we are and who we want to be as United Methodists. Of course, how you respond will depend on where you stand. If you hail from Baltimore, you might see things one way. If you are from Maputo, you will see things another way. Our points of view naturally differ as we are undeniably shaped by how, when, and where we grew up. That's just the way it is.

Perhaps you've seen Chimamanda Ngozi Adichie's much-quoted TED talk. If you want to check it out, go to: https://www.ted.com/talks/chimamanda_adichie_the_danger_of_a_single_story. She reminds us that, for many, the temptation is to think that ours is the only story or that our way of seeing is the only way. Adichie says there is danger in that. I tend to agree with her because it's been true in my experience.

Next Sunday morning, stand next to the pulpit and hold up the Bible, or any book, for that matter. The people in the first few rows will clearly see the front of the book. Those behind you in the choir will see the back. The organist might catch a glimpse of the spine. They all see different parts; some will see better than others, but they will all "fill in" what they see with what they expect to find. We see what we expect. We use our limited view to posit how the whole thing looks, the whole Bible as well as the whole story. We intuit motives and anticipate outcomes. But we see dimly; only later will we clearly see face to face.

This study guide comes out of the conviction that the church is thirsty for in-depth theological conversation and discernment. Just as Jesus offered the woman at the well living water, which she mistakenly took to mean only deep well water, so too he extends that invitation to us. Let us understand the true nature of God's gifts to us. Let us take up his invitation and drink living water together. This study guide is an opportunity to see differently and fill in, using the rich and varied vantage points of others. The results might be surprising and even refreshing. They might even make new openings for God. But one thing is for sure. If we seek the truth together and love God together, we will venture into the arms of Christ.

Dr. Kim Cape, General Secretary
General Board of Higher Education and Ministry
The United Methodist Church

The Conversation Matters

But as he which hath called you is holy,
So be ye holy in all manner of conversation.
—I Peter 1:15 (KJV)

This study guide is an introduction into a conversation that may well affect the future of The United Methodist Church as we know it. Whether we want to acknowledge it or not, our church is at a fork in the road, and how we go forward or whether we go forward together as a denomination is at stake. Our history brings us to this significant moment, and for whatever reason, the issues at hand involve inclusion of particular groups of people. Even naming some of these groups, however, is fraught with difficulty; but for the sake of this guide, we shall refer to these people in the same manner as does our *Book of Discipline*. But in so naming let us not forget that, as the people called Methodists, we believe all persons are made in God's image and that God's grace is for all and available to all. Let us also not forget that United Methodist members, whether from the LGBTQ (Lesbian, Gay, Bisexual, Transgender, Queer)[1] community or the Good News Movement, from

---

1   Nomenclature regarding gender and sexual minorities continues to change. A helpful guide is *National Geographic*, vol. 231:1 (January 2017). This special issue is titled "Gender Revolution."

Macedonia, Mozambique, or the United States, are Christians who have taken vows to be faithful members of The United Methodist Church with their time, talents, gifts, service, and witness. And as United Methodists we share the mission—to make disciples of Jesus Christ in order to transform the world.

For as long as there has been a church, human sexuality and related social conventions and institutions have been discussed issues. Jesus taught about marriage (Matthew 19:4-6; Mark 10:6-9); Paul wrote about human intimacy and human relationships (Romans 1:26-27; Ephesians 5; 1 Corinthians 7:1-16; Colossians 3:18-19). No matter how you interpret these and other biblical passages, the Bible does not shy away from portraying us as human in all our glory and infamy (Psalm 8:5, we are created a little lower than the angels; Mark 15:24, Jesus is executed by Roman crucifixion). We can count on the Bible to give us an honest look at who we are; and yet, with God's help we see who we can be as individuals and as a community of faith. So like the biblical writers, we should not hesitate or be afraid of looking squarely at who we are and who we can be as faithful, thinking Christians, even when we are divided and disagree, even, at times, when we disagree profoundly.

It would be foolish not to acknowledge that we United Methodists are divided in our thinking about homosexuality and whether or not our church should ordain practicing homosexuals. This study guide presents to United Methodists an opportunity to consider what has become a cultural and ecclesial flashpoint—the nexus of tangled issues related to human sexuality.

This resource is the fruit of colloquy from a specific event entitled The Unity of the Church and Human Sexuality: Toward a Faithful United Methodist Witness, a collaboration between the General Board of Higher Education and Ministry, the American Association of United Methodist Theological Schools, and the

Commission on a Way Forward. Candler School of Theology hosted this event March 9–12, 2017, and the dean of Candler School of Theology, Dr. Jan Love, kicked off the colloquy reminding everyone that conversation matters and conversation at this event matters more than most.

The participants of this colloquy were international United Methodist scholars from United Methodist seminaries[2] and Asbury Theological Seminary; also included were United Methodist scholars from Mozambique and Copenhagen, Denmark. The following pages of this small book will refer to the plenary paper given by Charles M. Wood, entitled "An Ecclesial Vision for The United Methodist Church," which is included in the appendix, but this resource will also refer to discussions and conversations from the colloquy.

At the colloquy participants presented papers that included descriptive and proscriptive analyses, such as Russell E. Richey's paper entitled "From Christmas Conference to General Conference Today's United Methodist: Living with/into Its Two Centuries of Regular Division"; Ted A. Campbell's essay "Grounds for Unity in The United Methodist Church and a Proposed Way Forward"; William J. Abraham's "In Defense of Mexit: Disagreement and Disunity in United Methodism," and Julio Andre Vilanculos's "United Methodist Church Unity and Human Sexuality: African Voices." There were historical perspectives, such as Anne Burkholder's "The Clash between Unity, Inclusion, and Covenant: Lessons from History," and essays that drew from biblical, theological, ethical, and ecclesiastical resources, such as Kenneth J. Collins's "Human Sexuality and

---

2 Boston University School of Theology; Candler School of Theology; Claremont School of Theology; Drew University Theological School; Duke University Divinity School; Gammon Theological Seminary; Garrett-Evangelical Theological Seminary; Iliff School of Theology; Methodist Theological School in Ohio; Perkins Theological Seminary; Saint Paul School of Theology; United Theological Seminary; Wesley Theological Seminary.

the Unity of the Church: Toward a Faithful United Methodist Witness." There were contributions from a variety of disciplines: for example, pastoral care–scholar Jeanne Hoeft, "Diversity, Identity, Contextuality, and Authentic Witness"; evangelism scholars such as Jack Jackson, "A Division of Heart: John Wesley's Case for Separation," and Mark R. Teasdale, "Quantity, Quality, and Balkanization: The Failure of Apostolic Mission Leading to the UMC's Current Deadlock over Human Sexuality"; and worship and liturgical theologians such as L. Edward Phillips, "Same-Sex Marriage, Just War, and the Social Principles: Grappling with the Incompatible." Some papers were theological, such as Kendall Soulen's "Is the Debate about Human Sexuality a Matter of *Status Confessionis*? Finding the Right Historical Analogy." Some papers were intensely personal, such as Karen Baker-Fletcher's paper, "Bodies That Touch," and Lisa M. Allen-McLaurin's paper, "Where Will You Go from Here?"

There is no doubt that these papers represent a wealth of knowledge and perspectives, for example Cathie Kelsey's "How Do United Methodists Know a Sin When We See It?"; Barry E. Bryant's "The Methodist Chimera and 'Execrable Villainies'"; Philip Clayton's "The Heart of Wesleyanism: Convergence and Divergence"; Morris L. Davis's "The Methodist Merger of 1939: Case Study in the Primacy of Christian Unity"; Christopher Evans's "Engaging the 'Public/Private' Split: United Methodism and Lessons from the Fundamentalist–Modernist Controversy"; Scott Kisker's "The Unity of the Church of God, The Body of Christ"; Sarah Heaner Lancaster's "Ecumenical Insights for Unity"; Kevin D. Newburg's "The Split That Didn't Happen"; Jørgen Thaarup's "The Unity of the Church in Relation to Christian Teaching and Human Sexuality"; Kevin M. Watson's "'Holiness of Heart and Life': Unity, Holiness, and the Mission of Methodism"; and Sondra Wheeler's "Remarks for Colloquy on Church Unity." Other participants included Jeffrey Conklin-Miller, Lallene J. Rector, and Elaine A. Robinson.

In small and large groups at the colloquy, the scholars discussed these and other topics related to the theme of human sexuality. They discussed, as Charles Wood asks, "How are we to find and live out an adequately diversified form of Christian community—one that could be a model and inspiration for an adequately diversified *human* community?"[3] We will not pretend that the issues are simple or that the colloquy papers are light reading. They represent United Methodist scholarship at its finest, well worth our time and energy. After the colloquy, scholars took the opportunity to revise their papers in order to reflect conversations with their peers. Toward the end of 2017, these important papers will be available as a book (please go to www.gbhem.org and watch for further details).

This colloquy, The Unity of the Church and Human Sexuality: Toward a Faithful United Methodist Witness, was in-

> How can we live out an adequately diversified form of Christian community?

---

3   See Charles M. Wood's colloquy paper "An Ecclesial Vision for The United Methodist Church" included appendix A.

> The United Methodist Church has a long tradition of holy conversation.

> "The best of all is God is with us."

tended to be a time of holy conversation. Here it must be added that we in The United Methodist Church have a long tradition of holy colloquy and conferencing. And when we present our best selves, United Methodists regard this kind of conversation as a means of grace—a way to experience the power and presence of the Holy Spirit. Indeed, this colloquy was much more than a dispersant group of intellectuals gathered to draw distinctions and debate ad nauseam. For some, it may have begun that way, but as the attending individuals listened to each other in small groups, sharing stories of the faith and the faithful, God showed up right on time. Does this mean that there was agreement about a way forward? No, but it did affirm that where two or more are gathered, God is in their midst. Yes, God was present. And yes, "The best of all is God is with us."[4]

As the colloquy progressed, a profound sense of grief and lament swept over some of those present, for the church that some regard as a mother who has nurtured us and affirmed our call to ministry is now ailing, possibly unto death. But as Kim Cape, General Secretary of the General Board of

---

4   John Wesley is reported to have said this on his deathbed.

Higher Education and Ministry, testified, God never leaves us to wallow in lament, because lament, as expressed in the Psalms, yields to hope—hope for a future into which God beckons us. In a related conversation after one of the colloquy sessions, Karen Baker-Fletcher was heard to say, "Why is there so much anxiety? Look to the Black Church. We have survived and will continue because God is faithful and can make a way out of no way." What is that way? At this present moment we do not know. But we trust that God's grace will heal us, guide us, reconcile us, sustain us, and faithfully lead us forward during this time of trial.

United Methodism has a long tradition of intellectual excellence. This colloquy was a way to claim that heritage. We do well to remember that our founder, John Wesley, was an Oxford don who lectured at the university. The scholars who participated in the colloquy and the many others who serve the church as extension ministers in higher education represent our brain trust. Through them we can learn to better love God with our minds. As these scholars gathered in Atlanta for the colloquy to tackle some of the most vexing and thorny issues with which The United Methodist Church continues to grapple,

United Methodism has a long tradition of intellectual excellence.

United

Methodists are

a *head, heart,*

but also a

hands people.

We want to

love God with

our minds and

serve in God's

mission to a

hurting world.

they exemplified loving God with their minds just as their thinking represented the wide diversity of thinking in our church. During the colloquy, these scholars covenanted to come together for a time of holy conversation. This study guide further extends the invitation for you to participate in this holy conversation in your own setting, because conversation matters.

At our core, we United Methodists are a *head, heart,* but also a *hands* people. For us, like Christians before us, we take seriously Jesus's command to love God with all our heart, soul, mind, and strength—our whole being, warts and all—and to love others as ourselves (Luke 10:27; Matthew 22:37). Inspired and empowered by the Holy Spirit, we put our faith into action through acts of kindness, justice, and mercy (James 2:14-26). This is in our Methodist DNA. We want to love God with our minds but also serve in God's mission to a hurting world. We want to put our informed beliefs and convictions into practice for the benefit of others, to all people. We want to embody God's grace so that the world will be transformed and conform to God's intent for our lives and our life together.

This book can be used as a four-week study to help you talk about what matters and what it means to be a faithful witness and loving servant in Christian mission regarding issues involving human sexuality. This resource invites you into deep waters of discernment, knowing that God walks with us even as God goes before us (and cleans up after us). Just as Jesus reached out his hand to Peter when Peter began to sink in the Sea of Galilee, so God reaches out to us (Matthew 14:22-34). Let us see this time for holy conversation as an opportunity both to recommit ourselves to claiming our identity as the Body of Christ and also to reaffirm our vows to offer our prayers, presence, gifts, service, and witness—not for personal gain or advantage but to transform the world.

> This resource invites you into deep waters of discernment, with faith that God walks with us.

Questions for Discussion

1. Share the last time you felt the power and presence of God in your church.

2. Share an experience of holy conversation. What makes holy conversation different from ordinary conversation?

3. What do you believe that Wesley meant when he said, "The best of all is God is with us"? As you reflect on this, share how God is present with you, your family, your church. How does God call forth the best in us as Christians?

4. Give one characteristic of your best self and how you are striving to walk the road to perfection.

5. Read Galatians 5:22-26. This passage in the CEB version of the Bible lists the fruit of the Spirit as love, joy, peace, patience, kindness, generosity, faithfulness, gentleness, and self-control. To enter into a conversation with other people about human sexuality, and homosexuality in particular, which of these do you need the most?

6. How up-to-date is your knowledge about human sexuality? For recent information about human sexuality and gender, see the January 2017 issue of *National Geographic* and the online article at the National Geographic website entitled "How Science Is Helping Us Understand Gender," http://www.nationalgeographic.com/magazine/2017/01/how-science-helps-us-understand-identity-gender. For data related to opinions about homosexuality, go to the Pew Research Center, http://www.pewresearch.org/topics/gay-marriage-and-homosexuality/. Both sources offer helpful information regarding different viewpoints within different demographics, including international attitudes. Please take a look at the findings.

7. How do you respond to the observation by one of the colloquy participants that his views about homosexuality changed after he witnessed the godly fruit in the lives of homosexuals he knew? Have your views about homosexuality changed over the years? What changed your thinking?

8. How do you understand what the Bible says about homosexuality and deciding who can be saved? See, for example, Romans 1:26-28; Jude 1:5-8; 1 Timothy 1:8-11; Galatians 3:27-29.

9. It is often said that United Methodists are divided on issues regarding homosexuality. How divided is your family, your church, perhaps even yourself?

10. Generally speaking, do you consider yourself a hopeful person? Hope often comes as a result of suffering a crisis then affirming as Christians that God is Lord of the future. Share a time when you needed and found hope, or perhaps hope found you. How hopeful are you about your future? How hopeful are you about your local church? How hopeful are you about your denomination?

Loving God with Our Mind Matters

He responded, "You must love the Lord your God with all your heart, with all your being, with all your strength, and with all your mind, and love your neighbor as yourself."

—Luke 10:27 (CEB)

uke tells us that "a certain legal expert stood up to test Jesus" (Luke 10:25 CEB). The King James Version says that "a certain lawyer stood up and tempted" Jesus by asking a question about eternal life, and Jesus responds by quoting Deuteronomy 6:5. However, he adds to it. Jesus adds "with all your mind." This addition doesn't change the meaning of his answer, but including "mind" does offer emphasis and promise. We are to be thinking, faithful people. And just as after his baptism Jesus answered the Tempter with scripture, here Jesus again meets temptation with his knowledge of scripture, thus embodying his call to love God with one's whole being. How do we respond when faced with adversity? Some might say that The United Methodist Church is being tested now and that issues related to human sexuality are a means by which who we are and our mission as a community of faith are being put on trial. We are at odds with each other. How will we respond?

But first a word about disagreements. At this point in history, our church is in serious conflict over issues related to homosexuality. As you might expect there are stages of disagreement. When, for example, two people disagree the first

Let us put on
the mind of
Christ together.

thing that often happens is that one thinks that the other just isn't listening, so they begin to talk louder. But when that doesn't work, one begins to think that the other doesn't really know; the other person is "stupid." So they proceed to educate each other. Perhaps they point to the Bible, bring out their favorite commentary, or refer to what the preacher said last Sunday. But they still disagree. Seeing that they can't educate one another, each comes to believe that the other person is just stupid. The facts are simply lost on the other person who must be incapable of understanding. With increasing frustration, the disagreement moves to another stage. Although we might admire that neither has given up on the other, both begin to think that if the other has the facts but still can't understand them and is stupid then maybe the problem is deeper. Could it be the other person is evil?

Some disagreements about homosexuality in our church are unfortunately at that level. Some of us think others of us are ignorant, stupid, and/or evil. No. *We just disagree.* Let us take a step back and put on the mind of Christ together.

This little book invites you to put on the mind of Christ as we discuss human sexuality and how we as a community of faith should respond. In Philippians 4:5, Paul says: "Let this mind be in you that was also in Christ Jesus" (NRSV). It is instructive to note that when Paul addresses *you*, he is talking not to you, the individual, but you, the body of believers. He uses the plural form of *you*. He says that we together must be of one mind with Jesus Christ, who was humble, obedient, and successful in bringing God's mission into clear view and who invites us into faithful and joyful living. After all, the kingdom of God is now, and we can easily miss out if we mire ourselves in argument. But more important, loving God with our minds allows us to draw closer, not only to each other but also to God.

Abba Dorotheus of Gaza was a monk at the monastery of Abba Serid. Around AD 540, he founded his own monastery and became abbot there. He is known for his instructions, later complied as *Directions on Spiritual Training*. The Roman Catholic and Eastern Orthodox Churches recognize him as St. Dorotheus the Hermit of Kemet. This sixth-century Christian has a teaching that can help us. He asks us to use our imagination and envision a large circle, a wheel. At the center is God; God is at the hub. Radiating out from God are an infinite

As we draw closer to God, we draw closer to each other.

15

We are meant to wonder, love, and praise God.

number of radii, the spokes. These are the different ways human beings live, so when they want to come closer to God, they walk toward the center of the circle. And as they draw closer to God, they draw closer to each other. Loving God with our minds draws us closer to God and to each other.

But drawing closer together does not necessarily draw us closer to God. Humans in lock step are not necessarily more Christ-like. Sometimes, they are simply a mob. No, Christ must be our aim. If we share in our aim and if our aim is Christ, we have a far less chance of missing the mark. That is one reason that we together must put on the mind of Christ. As Paul reminds us, Christ is our head (Colossians 1:18).

So let us draw together to think as a community of faith. But together let us put on the mind of Christ as we do so. The results will be we'll draw closer to God and to each other. There will be no reason for one to accuse the other of being ignorant or evil. Loving God with our mind matters at this juncture of being the Church—matters very much.

In this session, we will look at Charles Wood's paper. In particular we'll examine what he says about the church from a United Methodist perspective.

If we want to talk about the unity of the church and being faithful Christians living in a covenant community, we must first know what we want to preserve and make better.

The Church: Sign and Servant[1]

According to John Wesley, humans are meant for wonder, love, and praise. And through the church we have a creaturely participation in the life of the triune God where we can experience this purpose. As Wesley puts it, we are created "in the image of God, and designed to know, to love, and to enjoy [our] Creator to all eternity."[2] This is our calling as was revealed to us in Jesus Christ and which empowers us through the Holy Spirit. From this, we can understand that the church is the sign and servant to this reality, the new creation.

> Through the church we participate in the life of God.

The church's job is to be a sign and servant to this new reality, the community of faith that God envisions for us. And what is this new reality? First, the saving love of God is meant for all people, not just a few or even those we might choose. The biblical warrant for this statement comes from 1 Timothy 2:4 (NRSV), which says God "desires everyone to be saved

---

1   Refer to Charles Wood's paper found in appendix A of this book, beginning on page 65.
2   See Wood's paper in appendix A for sources. This refers to page 69, footnote 19.

The saving love of God is for all people.

The saving love of God transforms.

and to come to the knowledge of the truth." Further Wood reminds us of John Wesley's comment on this scripture from his *Explanatory Notes upon the New Testament*, which emphasizes the word "everyone." This leads directly into Wesley's understanding of God's grace, which while extended to all does not override human freedom. Rather, God's grace activates it. It makes us response-*able*, so that our salvation is a gift but it also involves our free participation.

Second, the saving love of God transforms. But transformation is not merely change; rather we are changed so as to be made right with God. As we accept God's grace, we are justified, restored into a right relationship with God, and we are sanctified; that is, our very being is renewed as we walk with God and grow deeper and come to experience more fully God's love for us as we embody that love in acts of mercy, love, compassion, and justice for other people. For Wesley, we experience the love of God here and now; and as a result, we live in the power of the Holy Spirit not just for ourselves but also for the benefit of others.

Third, the love of God creates community. God reaches out through prevenient grace that makes us responseable. As we accept God's grace, we are restored to a right relationship with God, such that we are transformed by the power and presence of God in our lives—not just for our own benefit, but for the benefit of others—so that they too can come into a deeper relationship with God. Therefore, it just makes sense given our humanness that we seek out others. Surprisingly, however, we may find ourselves in communion with those we least expect to associate. Perhaps we find ourselves like Jesus in the homes of less-than-respectable people (rich or poor) and people shunned by society.

For Wesley, being in community and association with other Christians as they minister together came to mean that they were *in connection*. A Lutheran friend once said that he couldn't understand why Methodists use the noun *connection* as a verb. For us *connection* is an action word, and this helps sum up what it means to be a Methodist. We are people on a mission. We were conceived as a movement and have birthed many more. As Charles Wood reminds us,

> Wesley and those in connection with him found themselves moving beyond the established norms of churchly behavior, and challenging the church, by their

God's love creates community.

own example, to enact more fully God's gift of community. Thus the term "connection" took on new resonances of meaning, as what Wesley called "social holiness"—the growth in love and in the other fruit of the Spirit that is possible only in community. (Appendix A, page 71)

> At its best, the church is characterized by *koinonia*. At its worst, we are called into accountability and repentance.

The Church: Visible and Invisible

However, while the church is both a sign and servant to a living-giving community organized for love, wonder, and praise, we have a spotty record. It doesn't take Charles Wood to remind us that, in regard to the church, we have a very human history of success and failure, growth and loss, separations and unions, and even hatred and love. Although the church may be the Body of Christ and called into being by God, it also reflects human sin and finitude.

At its best, the church is characterized by *koinonia*, which is that communion created and sustained by the Holy Spirit, the invisible church. We might go further and say that there is also a distinction between two aspects of the visible church, as Charles Wood suggests (appendix A, page 74): the church as the *community of salvation* and the *community of witness*. The church as

20

we know it is called to be both: a community in which persons are coming to fullness of life and a community with a mission to be Christ's witnesses in the world.

We might say that in a way, the church is both human and divine. When we experience the presence of the living God during worship, at prayer, on retreat, or while serving in the soup kitchen, we are experiencing *koinonia*, surrounded by a cloud of witnesses. But while we are voting at Annual or General Conference, making pastoral appointments, or meeting to plan this year's stewardship ministry, we are also engaged in very human endeavors, making it all the more important to put on the mind of Christ, so that our efforts can be transformed by the power and presence of God who promises to be in the midst of us.

The Church: Faithful Witness
The church brings the saving grace of God by restoring human beings to their rightful vocation, so they too can live lives of wonder, love, and praise. And the church is called to be a faithful witness to God and God's purposes. As Wood points out (appendix A, page 75), this has something to do with faith, hope, and love, and a particularly Wesleyan way of approaching this is through an understanding of the threefold office of Christ—in traditional language,

> God calls the church to be a faithful witness to God and God's purposes.

Jesus's saving work as prophet, priest, and king. In his prophetic office, Christ brings us the truth. In his priestly office, he heals our relationship with God. In his kingly office, Christ guides and empowers us toward fullness of life in community. Wood says:

> The church, through it proclamation of the Word, its celebration of the sacraments, and the ordering of its common life, bears witness to what God has done and is doing through Jesus Christ and in the power of the Holy Spirit. (appendix A, page 75)

But the church will always be an ambiguous mixture of its history and present experience.

> The Spirit is mixed up in it [the church], and we do not know what it looks like until it is already before us. Nobody invented the . . . church, nor would anybody have invented it in the form in which it evolved. It could not have emerged without builders, of course, for which reason there was and is much that is human about it, sometimes for good, sometimes not. But the Lord also builds the house. (See Appendix A, page 78, footnote 25).

The church is a gift of the triune God to us.

The Church: Love Incarnate

The church is a gift of the triune God. Gift giving brings joy to the giver and the recipient. And just like at Christmas, it is always so much fun to watch loved ones unwrap gifts. Opening the gift of the church must also give God joy. As Wood says, "It is *God's gift* to us, but it is God's gift *to us*, and we have the freedom and the responsibility that comes with being recipients of such a gift." When God gave the church, God had us—you and me—in mind.

We know why God gives. Jesus tells us:

> For God so loved the world that he gave his only Son, so that everyone who believes in him may not perish but may have eternal life. Indeed, God did not send the Son into the world to condemn the world, but in order that the world might be saved through him. (John 3:16-17 NRSV)

Our role as a church is to give God's love away, as often and as much as we can. One way that we as United Methodists incarnate love is described in our theological task in the *Discipline*. (See appendix A, page 80.)

"The theological task," the *Discipline* says,

> though related to the Church's doctrinal expressions, serves a different function. Our doctrinal affirmations assist us in the discernment of Christian truth in ever-changing contexts. Our theological task includes the testing, renewal, elaboration, and application of our doctrinal perspective in carrying out our calling "to spread scriptural holiness over these lands." (Appendix A, page 80, footnote.16)

23

Let us find new ways to be the church so that all may live in wonder, love, and praise.

By their very character and content, our doctrinal standards not only permit but require the sort of responsible, thoughtful critical engagement that "Our Theological Task" describes. Our theological work must be "both critical and constructive," "both individual and communal," "contextual and incarnational," and "essentially practical." (Appendix A, page 80, footnote 17)

Conclusion

As the people called Methodists, we are faithful disciples who are a sign and servant of God's actions in the world. We stand with one foot planted in the sinking sand of our misguided, self-concerned, power-hungry human world but with the other held fast and secure by a God who will not let us go. We are called to be faithful witnesses and responsible actors in God's plan to reconcile the world to Godself and to incarnate God's love and saving grace to all people. As we put on the mind of Christ together, let us think of new ways to be the church to more people in more places so that all may live in wonder, love, and praise.

Questions for Discussion

1. Share a time when you loved God with your mind. Is it possible for you to put on the mind of Christ with persons with whom you disagree?

2. Read and discuss Philippians 4:5.

3. What new thing is God doing in your life? In your church's life? What new thing would you like God to do? Take a few minutes and pray about it.

4. How are you being a faithful, thoughtful disciple? How does your church help? How do thoughtful Christians respond to conflicts over human sexuality? Please give examples.

5. Why is being a thoughtful Christian important for you as an individual, as a church member and/or leader?

6. Every church has conflict. How do you seek to address conflict? at home? at church? Do you avoid it, confront it, gossip about it, let someone else handle it, blame someone, get angry and walk away? What works best when addressing conflict in your experience? What happens when people go from being ignorant to being evil? Share a time when your church overcame conflict.

7. It is often said that people are not usually convinced with facts, especially if their facts differ from yours. What has been your experience? What's the best way to change someone's mind? When was the last time you changed your mind about something or someone?

8. Why do we value education in the church? Share some things about God you have recently learned.

9. If being the church means we believe that God's grace is for all people and that we participate in God's transforming love that creates community, how does your local church stack up? How loving is your church? How do you know? How does it show?

10. How does your church, your Annual Conference, the General Church faithfully witness and incarnate love?

11. How can your church be more like the community of faith that God intends? Name ways that your church, your team, your class, your committee puts on the mind of Christ together. How can prayer and Bible study help? What resources might you need?

12. What is the relationship between social witness and spreading scriptural holiness? What does it mean to spread scriptural holiness? What different does it make?

13. What is the difference between knowing God and knowing about God? Share some examples.

14. How can you see God at work in dealing with issues related to human sexuality?

The United Methodist Church Matters

*Now among those who went up to worship
at the festival were some Greeks.
They came to Philip, who was from Bethsaida in Galilee,
and said to him, "Sir, we wish to see Jesus."*
—John 12:20-21 (NRSV)

Perhaps your local church is rocking along just fine. Perhaps your church neither cares nor is worried about the "goings on" in the denomination. Perhaps how the church thinks about homosexuals does not concern you, or perhaps you've made up your mind about the way forward. If so, you are probably not reading this little book. But no matter what you believe about homosexuality, it needs to be said that the mission of your church and of The United Methodist Church matters.

As the Bosnian War began to wind down in 1995, Methodists there decided to hold their Annual Conference. Given the size of the usual crowd, the planners rented a small hall. However, when the Conference opened, there were long lines of people waiting to get in. Who were these people, and where did they come from? As it turned out, most of the people were local Muslims. When asked why they wanted to attend a Christian church conference, it's reported that one man said, "You were here at the beginning of this conflict. You stayed when others left. You cared for our children, our families, and our soldiers when no one else would take them in. You said

Our mission: to make disciples for Jesus Christ for the transformation of the world.

you did it in the name of your God. We are here to meet your God."

Robert Kohler, a retired Assistant General Secretary of the Board of Ordained Ministry, was teaching a course in Christian Ethics to a group of Methodist pastors in Sofia, Bulgaria, when the War in Kosovo broke out. Suddenly there was great anxiety among the pastors when an errant missile landed not far from where they were meeting. All of the pastors were away from their homes, unsure whether or not their families were safe. Realizing their depth of concern, Kohler asked the pastors about the critical ethical issues they faced in their homes, their churches, their communities, their nation, and the world. When he had asked these questions to pastors in the United States, the responses were usually focused on sexuality, honesty, integrity, abuse of power, and so forth, and Kohler expected similar responses in Sofia. What he discovered, however, was that the ethical issues with which we are preoccupied in the United States were of little concern to these pastors from Bulgaria and Macedonia.

In fact, there was only one issue that preoccupied their thinking, and that issue was "hospitality," caring for the strangers who were now flooding over their borders to safety. Methodist families were taking strangers into their homes; Methodist churches were opening their doors to provide food and shelter; and communities were reaching out to meet the needs of refugees. Their nation was establishing camps for those who were on the move, and the person chosen to oversee the camps was a Methodist lay leader who would later inspire the pastors to live out their Wesleyan heritage through their acts of Christian hospitality.

We can learn much about caring for the strangers in our midst by looking at this example of a small group of Methodists in a small country, doing whatever they could to care for their neighbors and the displaced during the onset of war; we, the people called Methodists, were there.

The United Methodist Church recognizes itself as a denomination, one whose mission is to make disciples for Jesus Christ for the transformation of the world. On this we can agree, but at its heart, when we say this we also mean that our job as a church is to bring people to see Jesus. And our prayer as a church should be that when people look at us, they see Jesus. We also can agree that we as United Methodists see ourselves as connectional. But as Russell Richey says in his book, *Methodist Connectionalism: Historical Perspectives*, our problem is that there "is no one concept of

People still want to see Jesus.

For United Methodists, *connection* is a verb.

connectionalism; or perhaps more accurately, there are many concepts of it" (quoted by Charles Wood, appendix A, page 85). Wood goes on to say: "Methodist use of the word 'connexion' arose in the eighteenth century and derived from the fact that certain religious societies in Britain were at that time considered legitimate or lawful if they were supervised by, or 'in connexion with,' an Anglican cleric."

John Wesley was just that, an ordained member of the Anglican Church. While the spelling of the term *connexion* morphed into *connection*, its meaning also changed. Now, we tend to think of *connection* as having to do with such things as interdependence, mutuality, consultation, and collegiality in sharing power. In Wesley's day, it meant being under Wesley's direction or under the direction of those appointed by him and later ordained by him, which was contrary to Anglican Church law. For those early Methodists, the connexion involved a strong central authority and an effective chain of command. And even today, if you look closely the tensions inherent in the connexion as opposed to our connection still exist. Are we primarily centrally controlled with an authorized chain of command, or are we interdependent, mutual, consultative, and power sharing? In truth, we hold both in tension.

In the early days, Methodism was a movement. Even after Methodism made its way to Colonial America, it was still not what we would call an independent organized body until after the American Revolution.[1] The United Methodist denomination we know today is the result of various predecessor bodies; most recently in 1968 the Evangelical United Brethren Church and the Methodist Church merged, both of which were the result of other earlier mergers. In fact, we might wonder what a denomination actually *is*. Charles Wood says that being a denomination is generally a uniquely American way of being church, although some roots may go back through English Protestantism to the Reformation (appendix A, page 88). Wood goes on to point out that not even all churches in the United States see themselves as a denomination. Catholics and Episcopalians regard themselves as members of a worldwide communion and have some difficulty matching their experience to that model. Wood says that even Baptists have some strong reservation about the

> Do United Methodists need to be a denomination?

---

1   For a concise history of American Methodism, see Russell E. Richey, Kenneth E. Rowe, and Jean Miller Schmidt, *American Methodism: A Compact History* (Nashville: Abingdon Press, 2012).

There are some things that only the General Church can do.

idea, maintaining that the local congregation is the real church. We might even say that some megachurches, independent missions, and nondenominational institutions have become de facto denominations because of their need for stability, organization, and authorized leadership.

It is also true that many people in local congregations move freely from church to church, from denomination to denomination, without much thought, except, for example, for which church has the best children's or youth programming. Many in local congregations may have the words "United Methodist" on their church sign but function like they are something else entirely, even a world unto themselves.

So, why have a denomination at all if it only serves the bureaucratic needs of a group of churches? Another question has come to the fore recently: Is the concept of denomination even a serviceable institutional form in a worldwide context?

Regarding the first question about whether there is a need for denominational structure, there are some things only the General Church can do. While this book is not about UM structure, it might be helpful to review the mission of the church as accomplished by one of the General Agencies. One criticism in the past of the General Agencies[2] has been that they do not connect closely enough to the church so that there is a gap between them and the church. In response, the General Agencies now engage in deep listening to the church and are responding accordingly; for example the General Board of Higher Education and Ministry has started an academic publishing program; more extensive leadership and training opportunities for collegiate ministry; and, most recent, global Clinical Pastoral Education.

Our church follows our Methodist tradition as instituted by John Wesley, who expected that the innate desire of the heart for repentance, once fulfilled through the saving mercy of Christ, would lead to a deeply informed and committed discipleship. Consequentially, he provided his followers with readings and instruction in the Bible and other texts that he deemed necessary to heal their souls and bodies. In addition to the hardships of itinerant preaching, Wesley expected his preachers to read and study, dictating for them their course of study. This was done so that the preachers, as well as the laity, might understand the depths of Christian faith rooted both in the heart and in the mind.

Here is a taste of what The United Methodist Church can do through, for example, GBHEM. GBHEM oversees

---

2   General Conference establishes general agencies (or churchwide agencies) to provide essential services and ministries beyond the scope of individual local congregations and annual conferences, and they are important for providing a common vision, mission, and ministry for the entire global church. General Conference and the Connectional Table share in oversight of agency programs and ministries. Each agency is governed by a board of directors whose members, both lay and clergy, are elected by jurisdictions and central conferences. Bishops, as assigned by the council, also share oversight on these boards. They are the General Board of Higher Education and Ministry; General Commission on Archives and History; General Board of Church and Society; United Methodist Communications; Discipleship Ministries; General Board of Global Ministries; General Board on Finance and Administration; Wespath (Pension and Health Benefits); Religion and Race; The Status and Role of Women; United Methodist Men; United Methodist Women; United Methodist Publishing House.

training and credentialing of ordained persons and helps persons discern their call to ministry. In addition, it provides loans and scholarships for higher education. The United Methodist Church through GBHEM also endorses a multitude of highly trained chaplains and pastoral counselors who serve in such places as the Armed Services, hospitals, counseling centers, prisons, police stations, and fire stations. Furthermore, GBHEM trains leaders as it serves and resources campus ministry and the Historic Black Colleges of The United Methodist Church. Not only does GBHEM oversee the Course of Study for local pastors around the world but, in some places, GBHEM has constructed roads so that pastors can attend these courses, as well as translated books so that pastors can read in their native language. GBHEM works with United Methodist educational institutions at all levels across the world. It especially provides access for people who would not otherwise be connected to the church or be able to take advantage of its benefits. Only a General Agency can bring together United Methodists from all over the world for an event like the colloquy.

If we look at the last forty years, The United Methodist Church has worked to create structures in many countries on several continents under vastly different social, cultural, political, and economic conditions. Issues related to being a worldwide denomination are especially germane to issues of homosexuality. Laws and attitudes about homosexuality vary depending on cultural contexts. In some places, homosexual practice is anathema. Performing a same-sex marriage is not only illegal in some places but also punishable by death.

As previously mentioned, for data related to opinions about homosexuality, go to the Pew Research Center, http://www.pewresearch.org/topics/gay-marriage-and-homosexuality/.

There you will find helpful information about the variety of viewpoints within different demographics, including international attitudes. Please take a look at the findings.

The colloquy stimulated much discussion about denominational structure. Several scholars suggested that there might be better ways to organize ourselves going forward, whether or not we come to agreement about homosexuality. As Charles Wood asks, "How are we to live out an adequately diversified form of Christian community—one that could be a model and inspiration for an adequately diversified *human* community?" (appendix A, page 92). Perhaps there are better ways we should consider. Some other organizational possibilities are laid out in the next chapter.

In his paper, Charles Wood tells of an address by Ted Campbell (also a colloquy participant) to the World Methodist Council in 2016. In his speech, Dr. Campbell asked, "Might there be ways to divide that might create new unities?" That is, might current issues that divide us also serve to drive us toward an opportunity for different and perhaps more significant partnerships with our Wesleyan and ecumenical partners, such as with The Christian Methodist Episcopal Church (CME) or African

> Are there new and better ways to be a denomination?

> No matter what our organization, we must not obscure people's view of Jesus.

Methodist Episcopal Church (AME). So, we ask along with Charles Wood, "Can we, by the grace of God, come up with a way to allow adequate diversification that does not involve division, and that, over time, permits a fuller realization of and witness to genuine unity?" (appendix A, page 92).

But however we structure ourselves, we matter as a denomination, no matter how we reconfigure ourselves. No matter what, God has a mission for us, the people called Methodists. So however we organize, we must not obscure people's view of Jesus. The United Methodist Church matters only to the degree that we bring people to the healing and wholeness that Jesus offers.

In response to the health crisis in Africa, a young American doctor went to serve on behalf of her church. She went under the auspices of an agency of The United Methodist Church. There she met an African doctor and his wife, who were also United Methodists. Over the course of a month, the American woman and her African counterpart worked side by side to heal and alleviate suffering.

Hours blurred into days until the month passed, and she was relieved by another doctor and went back home. Being inspired and energized by her work, she planned to return to Africa a second time. Upon her arrival, she reunited with the African doctor, and this time she met another of his wives. With no time to think about it, she and the African doctor drove over the countryside curing victims and saving many lives. Many called her an angel sent from God. Many called him God's healing hands. Then, as before, time came for her to go home. When she returned, she found to her delight that her state had just legalized same-sex marriage, and she married her partner of many years. Not long after the ceremony, she accepted another tour of duty serving in Africa; she returned, this time meeting yet another of the African doctor's wives. Given that he had to have at least three wives, she decided to confront her colleague, and in so doing, she told him about her recent marriage to her same-sex partner. They both looked at each other horrified—he at the thought that his friend was a lesbian and therefore worthy of death, and she at the thought of the injustices of polygamy. Then they asked each other: "What is more important, doing the work of God together or being imperfect, even sinful, vessels?" The truck door slammed and off they went.

The people the doctors helped and healed saw Jesus in them. What do you see?

Questions for Discussion
1. In whose face have you seen Jesus recently? How do you recognize the face of Jesus in others?

2. Share what it means to be a United Methodist. How did you become a United Methodist?

3. What is your understanding of the mission of your church? the denomination?

4. What kinds of missions have you been involved with? Share some about your most meaningful experience of being in mission.

5. Share a story about your experience of the United Methodist connection.

6. How connected is your church to your conference, your community, the denomination?

7. Do you think that the days of denominations are over?

8. What does it mean to be a worldwide church structure? What advantages and disadvantages are there in being a worldwide denomination?

9. Are there other ways to organize The UMC that might be more helpful in dealing with diversity?

10. If The UMC were to split, what would happen to ordination, endorsement, educational oversight, global mission, colleges and universities, and other institutions that are affiliated with The UMC?

11. If The UMC were to split or splinter, what might happen to your local church? What might happen to United Methodist mission in your district? Annual Conference? the world?

12. Make a list of mission work that The UMC does. What would you like to know about the General Agencies and their work? How can they help you?

Finding a Way Forward Matters

God is love, and those who abide in love
abide in God, and God abides in them.
Love has been perfected among us in this:
that we may have boldness on the day of judgment,
because as he is, so are we in this world.
There is no fear in love, but perfect love casts out fear.
—1 John 4:16b-18a (NRSV)

Pursue peace with everyone,
and the holiness without which no one will see the Lord.
See to it that no one fails to obtain the grace of God;
that no root of bitterness springs up and causes trouble
and through it many become defiled.
—Hebrews 12:14-15 (NRSV)

D r. Kim Cape tells this story:

In 2001, I went to South Africa and Mozambique as staff for *The Upper Room*, a daily devotional guide. I was working for Steve Bryant, who was to preach the Evensong service that afternoon. We were there to start the African Portuguese version of the magazine, so we traveled north from Maputo up the coast on the one paved, one-lane road, visiting churches and asking people to share their stories of God as we went. We rode for several hours, occasionally jolting and quickly

> Everyone has a story, some meant to be shared, others never to be told.

swerving on the narrow shoulder of the road, dodging potholes. As I lazily gazed out the window, I noticed what I thought was orange construction tape along the road. When we swerved right, I could almost reach out and touch it. But we kept going and kept going for miles and miles, and the orange tape stretched ahead of us like a long ribbon. Then, suddenly I shook my head in a realization. There wasn't any construction anywhere. So I asked the driver what was going on with all the orange tape. And he casually answered, "Oh, that orange tape is there to show where the landmines are. They're still many landmines in the fields left over from our civil war." You can imagine that I didn't doze off again. Landmines were everywhere.

Landmines are everywhere, especially when it comes to conversation, even holy conversation, about human sexuality. Why? Perhaps because everyone has a story, some meant to be shared, others never to be told. But whatever the case when discussing homosexuality and the church, we must stay alert. Charles Wood reminds us that many times people are simply not interested in seeking or promoting mutual understanding (appendix A, page 93). Why is that the case? Sometimes we seek to avoid or prevent understanding. And we possess tools for that purpose. Of these, fear is one of the most accessible and potent, and this probably accounts for the hundreds of times God and/or his agents say in the Bible: "Fear not." Fear and suspicion put us on the defensive rather than opening a way forward. We are all too familiar with "wedge issues" and polarizing strategies in churches as well as in society as a whole. It is up to us to move beyond our fears and anxieties to a deeper faith and a more perfect love of God and neighbor.

During one of the large group discussions at the colloquy, Dr. Lisa M. Allen-McLaurin made the comment that we, the church, cannot be in the business of throwing people away. She did not reference Jesus's parable of the Good Samaritan, but she didn't need to. The meaning was clear. No matter what position you take regarding homosexuality, the church needs all people. It takes all of us to make and nurture disciples of Jesus Christ to transform the world.

Dr. Cape also tells this story:

> My father-in-law, John Gibbs, was born in Seguin, a small town in South Texas. His mother died in childbirth, so he never knew her. His father worked in Austin and spent most of his time there, meaning that John was reared by his two maiden aunts. John recalled that when he was in high school and ready to leave for a date, he'd have to walk by his aunts who would be sitting at the kitchen table—usually shelling pecans or black eyed peas—and before the screen door shut behind him, no matter how fast he tried to escape, Aunt Bess would say, "John, remember who you are kin to."

We may need something new. We may need to redefine what a denomination is.

As United Methodists we are kin to all Christians and part of the Church universal. Not only that, but we are also surrounded by a great cloud of witnesses (Hebrews 12:1) who are urging us forward, encouraging us to persevere and run the race that is before us. Human conflicts will not defeat God's mission or alter the divine plan to reconcile all the world to God. So who are we to give up now and simply turn our back on The United Methodist Church and walk away?

If you think human sexuality is a serious threat to the unity of The United Methodist Church, you might find how the Church faced another threat and found greater unity by formulating the Nicene Creed. Briefly put, in AD 325 Emperor Constantine convened a council of bishops to settle a controversy that posed a danger to the Church. The debate was over the divine and human nature of Jesus Christ. The conversation was less than holy, and blood literally ran in the streets. It seemed that there were no words to adequately express the divinity and humanity of Christ, or at least not any that all could agree upon. That is until Athanasius of Alexandria used a new word, *homoousios*; and while not perfect, it was good enough.

Today, The United Methodist Church is threatened. In fact, some local churches have already withdrawn from the denomination over issues related to human sexuality. In his paper, Charles Wood suggests that we need something new. We need to redefine what a denomination is, so that our church can "allow adequate diversification that does not involve division, and that, over time, permits a fuller realization of and witness to genuine unity" (appendix A, page 92). Is this even possible? To answer, Dr. Wood describes four concepts that might help: subsidiarity, reconciled diversity, differentiated consensus, and reception (appendix A, pages 93-98).

Subsidiarity

Subsidiarity is the principle that decisions are made on the lowest possible level. While the word "level" might be off-putting to some, it seems unavoidable as a notion of hierarchy is built into the word itself. Another way of putting it might be to say "in the most specific context allowable." Or perhaps: *subsidiarity* is a principle that consists in not taking from individuals the tasks with which they are able to undertake on their own and avoiding the transfer of decision-making to higher authorities who are not immediately concerned. This principle can be used to privilege local church or local ministry context.

Wood goes on to say that one advantage to subsidiarity is that people usually find it much easier to work toward mutual understanding when the effort does not involve an internal struggle over resources and power. The larger the context, often the larger the stakes; and when decisions generate conflict, it's easier to de-escalate the tensions. This may help people be more open and satisfied with outcomes for the long term.

Reconciled Diversity

Dr. Wood explains that reconciled diversity is, "in a way, subsidiarity after the fact" (appendix A, page 95). This principle

> We are being reconciled by God despite our differences.

is used by the Community of Protestant Churches in Europe to designate the way that churches with historically conflicting ways of ordering themselves, that is, with different structure of ordained ministry and oversight, can recognize each other's order as legitimate, although not binding on themselves. Wood goes on to say that this principle applies to diversity in official doctrine and doctrinal standards: "It does not come about because we have decided to overcome our divisions, but because God is not allowing our division to have the last word" (appendix A, page 95).

For United Methodism at this point in our history, Wood says that reconciled diversity may sound as if we are content to "agree to disagree" and no longer explore the questions on which we differ. Again, it is not our differences that are reconciled, but rather that we are being reconciled by God despite our differences.

Differentiated Consensus

This principle describes the way churches with seemingly conflicting teachings, through a process of sharing and discernment, find that they are not actually in conflict. They find a more fundamental principle in which to appeal. Here different parties can maintain their differences and yet understand themselves as affirming that the other can also affirm.

Might this principle be helpful to The United Methodist Church? Might there be a more fundamental principle that can subsume those who want to ordain self-avowed practicing homosexuals and those who do not? This depends on how the debate is framed, and the colloquy papers framed the issues differently, making differentiated consensus unlikely at this point.

Reception

This principle is as old as the Church itself and it is closely connected with the theme of conciliarity, which refers to the way in which decisions are reached in council—a synod, assembly, or gathering of representative Christian leaders—for example, General Conference. The importance of reception is that a relatively minor regional counsel may come to be regarded as authoritative if its teaching comes to be widely accepted.

Perhaps not being received is instructive. Some of the decisions concerning homosexual practice, for example, have not been received, at least in a positive manner by significant numbers of United Methodist members, clergy, Annual Conferences, and bishops. And this leads us back to the reason our church is where we find ourselves today.

Suggestions for New Structures[1]

During the colloquy, some suggestions for new configurations of what is now The United Methodist Church came forward. These are two. There were others.

Conciliar Fellowship Model

Conciliar fellowship is another term currently in use in ecumenical discussion to describe the situation that enables churches to structure as a "community of communities." Adopting

---

1   These models come out of one small group's conversation during the colloquy and were submitted by Dr. Kendall Soulen, who was the group facilitator. These are included to spur the reader's imagination. They are not and were not meant to be proposals.

> The instruments of conciliar fellowship are essentially . . . Word, Sacrament, and Order.

(more fully and intentionally) a conciliar model as part of a way forward for The United Methodist Church would enable us to envision our "connectionalism" in terms of the conditions for conciliar fellowship. The instruments of conciliar fellowship are essentially the same as the instruments of Christian unity; this is Word, Sacrament, and Order. When applied to the situation of separated Christian communities in ecumenical discussion, these have commonly been articulated so as to make explicit some conditions for overcoming barriers to unity. A representative and short list of the conditions for conciliar fellowship would thus include these things: shared confession of the apostolic faith, mutual recognition of members and ministries, shared celebration of the Eucharist, an ability to meet and make decisions together when appropriate, and cooperation in mission. The question, however, remains whether The United Methodist Church, with some adjustments in polity, procedures, and ways of relating, enables us to meet these conditions, in which case we would be in conciliar fellowship within the connection; or, whether we will have to accept that we are, at best, at a "preconciliar" stage, that is, unable to fulfill one or more of these conditions.

In addition, there are degrees or levels of preconciliarity, ranging from things such as local or national councils of churches to things like concordats and "full communion" relationships. If the church were to opt for preconciliarity, we would have to decide just what degree or level would be appropriate. For those members of the church who decide that their differences from others are such that they cannot regard the others as genuine Christians—that is, that these others are denying something that they take to be essential to Christian faith and life—even a relationship of preconciliarity would not be possible at this point.

Preconciliar Model

The notion of the preconciliar option has come into focus in ecumenical discussions where churches cannot yet exercise the conciliar option of being a communion of communions due to irreconcilable differences in Word, Sacrament, or Order. Yet it holds open the door for progress to that option.

Using this model it would be possible for a United Methodist Council of Churches to form to which the successor denominations to the current United Methodist Church could be affiliated. The council could be an association of new United Methodist bodies (potentially two or three). It would not have oversight or authority over the autonomous new bodies but would provide a bond of union stronger than, say, the World Council of Churches. Hence it would be an institutional site that could facilitate joint projects that would benefit member churches. This could well include joint study projects to tackle the many complex issues around human sexuality. Its raison d'etre would be to secure a genuine bond of fellowship between any new instantiations of United Methodism.

Member churches could be in full communion with each other, recognizing in each other sufficient commonality in terms of the apostolic faith, Word, Sacrament, and ministry to express this in terms of membership in the United Methodist Council of Churches. There could be full communion and recognition of each other's members and ministries, akin to current arrangements with the Evangelical Lutheran Church in America (ELCA) and Episcopal Church (pending). Transfer of members would require the orderly transfer of membership and clergy, provided the disciplinary requirements of the receiving body be satisfied. Each church could have its own bishops and its own *Book of Discipline*. Each could be responsible for its own funding.

The rationale for this option faces the fact that we are already in a state of disunity or internal separation due to irreconcilable differences related to Word, Sacrament, and Order. However, it keeps intact the recognition of each other as Christian communions. It frees each church to follow its own identity, and, given that identity is related to vitality, it provides the possibility of a new lease on life for each communion. It furnishes the possibility of provoking one another to love and good works. It also keeps open the door for a move to full conciliarity in the future. Likewise, it could open the option of other Methodist churches around the world to affiliate with the United Methodist Council of Churches.

Conclusion

Whatever future God has for The United Methodist Church, of this we can be certain: Christ is Lord. Christ is Lord of the past, present, and future. So what have we to fear?

When traveling in Mozambique, Dr. Kim Cape and several others arrived at a church. They had been on the road many hours and were tired and hungry. There they were met by about forty people, who welcomed the guests with clapping and singing. The singing was angelic, like God's own choir. In the subsequent meeting, Dr. Cape and the other visitors told the people that they wanted to hear their stories of God and that they wanted to share those stories as a witness to the faith. The church people were delighted, and one man said, "We are so happy you asked us to share our stories of God. We have many stories to tell. We have had war; we have had flood and sickness and famine. And we have many stories to tell of how good God has been to us. But first let us eat."

The women of the church had prepared lunch for the four Americans, the district superintendent and his wife, the pastor and his wife, and the lay leader. There were nine people who would share in the meal. The women brought out a platter of roast chicken and fried potatoes. Kim counted the pieces of chicken. There were five whole chickens, cut in half—ten pieces of chicken—and no silverware. The pastor reached out and grabbed half a chicken, tore it apart and said, "We eat Mozambique style." So Kim grabbed her chicken and started eating. But as she did, she noticed the members of the congregation. There were men sitting on benches, women on the dirt floor, and other women passing through the crowd. These women had wooden bowls and were spooning out rice, over which they poured a little chicken broth. Kim said, seeing this, "It got harder to chew." Finally, there was one half chicken left, and the pastor took

On this we agree: Christ is Lord.

it and passed it down for the guests to share. Then Kim realized, as she ate her chicken, "This wasn't a Tyson's chicken. This chicken had run for his life a long time." And she pictured the United Methodist Women gathering that morning deciding whose chickens would be lunch. Kim says, "That five-chicken dinner was a sacramental act of hospitality, but it was also an act of sacrificial giving. At that moment, it was clear that the host was Jesus Christ. Christ was the honored one. It was for Christ they gave their best. Their all."

As we United Methodists gather to think of new ways to be a worldwide church, we must be willing to give Jesus our best, our all. As we seek to be faithful United Methodists, who at the moment are divided over human sexuality, we must be prepared to give and extend hospitality to guests, foreigners, strangers, friends, neighbors, and family. Because Christ is the host. Christ is the head of the church, and we have vowed to give our time, service, gifts, talents, and witness to make disciples of Jesus Christ for the transformation of the world.

As we think about our church and put on the mind of Christ together, consider this poem attributed to Ernest Campbell, who was senior pastor of Riverside Church in New York City from 1968–1976.

> To be young is to study in schools
> we did not build.
> To be mature is to build schools
> In which we will not study.
>
> To be young is to swim in pools
> we did not dig.
> To be mature is to dig pools
> in which we will not swim.

To be young is to sit under trees,
which we did not plant.
To be mature is to plant trees
under which we will not sit.

To be young is to dance to music
we did not write.
To be mature is to write music
to which we will not dance.

To be young is to worship in churches
we did not build.
To be mature is to build churches
in which we may not worship.

As we go forth as a church, let us covenant together to love God with our minds and accept God's grace to live as mature Christians lost in wonder, love, and praise.

Questions for Discussion

1. How important is your church to you? How important is being United Methodist? In your opinion, does The United Methodist Church matter? If so, how much?

2. How do you keep your membership vows to serve God with your prayers, presence, gifts, service, and witness? What does holiness mean to you?

3. What landmines have you found in talking with others about human sexuality? Who in your church agrees and who disagrees with your stance toward homosexuality practice?

4. These days there seems to be many different genders and some transgendered people. Is this an issue in your church? If it is an issue or might become an issue, how will your church address it?

5. What are some "wedge" issues that you've experienced? How have they divided your church, your family, your own thinking?

6. What kind of listener are you? Share a time when you felt heard. What was it like? What happens when someone does not feel heard? What ways can we better hear people with whom we disagree?

7. Take some time and think about ways The United Methodist Church might better serve people who feel strongly about human sexuality, whether for or against?

8. Discuss subsidiarity, reconciled diversity, differentiated consensus, and reception. How might these principles help move the church forward? Can you think of other helpful principles?

9. How would your church react if your bishop appointed a practicing homosexual to your church? What would you do?

10. Do you know someone who is homosexual or part of the LGBTQ community?

11. Consider the Pew Research. How do you respond to the fact that homosexual practice is becoming more accepted? Does it matter? See: http://www.pewresearch.org/fact-tank/2016/05/12/support-steady-for-same-sex-marriage-and-acceptance-of-homosexuality/.

12. Do you know someone who is a practicing homosexual and is also a faithful Christian? What difference does it make?

13. Do you see a way forward for The United Methodist Church? How do you respond to the Conciliar Fellowship model and the Preconciliar model? What are the strengths and weaknesses of each?

14. How important is it to you that The UMC remain one denomination? How important is it to your church's mission? to the denomination's mission? What if separation from the church destroys local congregations? What if continuing as we are as a denomination hurts people and destroys local congregations?

15. Are you willing to offer hospitality to those with whom you have conflict? Are you willing to sacrifice for their benefit? How might that look?

16. What do you believe is God's will for the future of The United Methodist Church?

17. How has your faith grown over the last year? Are there other people you know who would welcome the opportunity to better love God with their minds?

Afterword

The colloquy The Unity of the Church and Human Sexuality: Toward a Faithful United Methodist Witness represented a collaboration between the General Board of Higher Education and Ministry, the American Association of United Methodist Theological Schools, and the Commission on a Way Forward. More personally, it began as a conversation with two friends, Dean Jan Love and Dr. Kim Cape. We saw the need for a collaborative response to the complex place in which the church finds itself in relation to LGBTQ identity and Christian unity.

The alternative to collaboration is our common practice of living in silos. When I served as a pastor, I would often hear the word *silo* in administrative meetings. One evening a lay member shared the dictionary definition of a silo's purpose: to keep the grain pure. Silos are often born in a spirit of protectiveness, but they can lead to isolation and even definition. There is a greater need, in the present moment, for the cross fertilization of ideas. We often say that we value diversity, but this does not always include cognitive diversity, a willingness to think in different ways. And this is imagination.

In his work on doctrine and theology, my professor Thomas Langford made the following distinction:

> Doctrine reflects the grasp of the church; theology reflects the reach of the church. To use another analogy: doctrine is the part of the cathedral already completed,

exploratory theology is creative architectural vision and preliminary drawings for possible new construction.[1]

Our usual ways of being together, as church and academy, are not serving us well. The end of deconstruction is finally a flattened world and a divided church. There is a greater need for new construction than deconstruction. My hope for the fruit of this scholarly work is that it will open new conversations, develop friendships among new conversation partners, and serve the Council of Bishops, the Commission on a Way Forward, the delegates to the next General Conferences, and our larger church.

It would be absurd to try to find a way forward apart from the intellectual life of the church. And this is why we gathered at Emory University, to reflect on the contribution of scholars from across a wide spectrum. If you are engaged in this conversation, leading a study group, serving a congregation, or engaging in a personal struggle, you are present to this same intellectual exercise.

I served as a pastor for twenty-eight years. I recall a Palm Sunday in one of those congregations. At the conclusion of the last service, two leaders asked to meet with me. They described what had happened in their Sunday School class that morning. Members John and Mary (names changed) had stood up before the lesson and made the statement, "Our son is gay, we love him, we do not like The United Methodist Church's statement about human sexuality, and we are leaving the church." And then they had left. The two leaders looked at me and said, "We think you should reach out to John and Mary."

Later that afternoon, I did. I called, and they welcomed me

---

1   Thomas A. Langford, "Doctrinal Affirmation and Theological Exploration," in *Doctrine and Theology in the United Methodist Church* (Nashville: Kingswood, 1991), 204.

to sit with them. I said, simply, "I am here to listen." And so for an hour they shared in personal and intense ways. Then there was a quietness, and Mary asked me, "What do you want to say?" Here is the response I was led to give. I said,

First, I want to thank you for the gift of listening to you. And second, I don't think you are leaving the church. I think if you were leaving you would have already departed. I think that by standing before the people who know you best, your friends, you were saying, this is who we are, this is important to us, and if you are going to know and love us, this is core to who we are. I think you will help the class grow over time, as you walk together, and I think they will help you.

In that moment this was not persuasive. But afterward, John and Mary were always present with their class. The relationships deepened. And years later, when John struggled and later died with an illness, the class surrounded and loved him, Mary, and their son.

I share this pastoral experience with the conviction that God calls us to lean into our differences and to listen more closely to our convictions. We are being led from our silos and divisions into creative collaboration and possible new construction.

Bishop Kenneth H. Carter Jr.

An Ecclesial Vision for The United Methodist Church

Dr. Charles M. Wood

Communion, whose source is the very life of the Holy
Trinity, is both the gift by which the Church lives and, at
the same time, the gift that God calls the church to offer to
a wounded and divided humanity in
hope of reconciliation and healing.
—*The Church: Towards a Common Vision*

We need forms of polity that are consistent with our core
convictions: that is, forms that honor the radically inclusive
scope of God's saving grace, forms that recognize and
build upon the transformative character of that grace, and
forms that will serve, rather than subvert,
the growth of genuine community.
—*Wonder, Love, and Praise*

The question for The United Methodist Church at this
juncture is a local parallel to the question that drives the
ecumenical discussion: How are we to find and live out an
adequately diversified form of Christian community—one
that could be a model and inspiration for an adequately
diversified *human* community?
—"An Ecclesial Vision for The United Methodist Church"

By action of the 2016 General Conference, a study document entitled *Wonder, Love, and Praise: Sharing a Vision of the Church*, prepared under the auspices of the Committee on Faith and Order of The United Methodist Church, is to be the basis of a church-wide study over the next four years.[1] My aim in what follows is to highlight some of what I take to be the principal points of that study document and to offer some reflections on the understanding of the unity of the church—of the church universal and of The United Methodist Church in particular—that might emerge from an engagement with it.

The Committee on Faith and Order is a relatively new thing, having been established by the General Conference in 2008. It was then inadvertently abolished by the 2012 General Conference, reconstituted provisionally by action of the Council of Bishops, and formally reestablished by General Conference action in 2016. The chief mandate of the committee, as I understand it, was and remains twofold: first, to engage in theological reflection on matters of faith and order on behalf of the church; and second, to encourage and support such theological reflection throughout the church.[2]

Of course, the term *faith and order* has a history of more than a century of usage in the ecumenical movement, where it has represented the two main elements of the ecumenical

---

1   The enabling legislation is found in Resolution #8007, "Study of Ecclesiology," *The Book of Resolutions of The United Methodist Church 2016* (Nashville: The United Methodist Publishing House, 2016), 676–77. The document is not mentioned there by name because it had not yet been translated and made available in the requisite official languages of the General Conference. Currently, the English version is available online at http://www.ocuir.org/wp-content/uploads/2016/06/Wonder_Love_and_Praise_final.pdf, and references to passages in it in this paper will be by line number in that version. Both the document itself and a study guide for it are to be made available at www.umc.org/CFOWonderLovePraise. The hope is that the document will be significantly improved in light of the reflection and response generated during the period of study.

2   *The Book of Discipline of The United Methodist Church 2016* (Nashville: The United Methodist Publishing House, 2016), ¶¶443–50.

goal of visible unity. Let me borrow from the ecumenical veteran Michael Kinnamon's "a short list of 'tangible signs of the new life of communion'": shared confession of the apostolic faith, mutual recognition of members and ministries, shared celebration of the Eucharist, an ability to meet and make decisions together when appropriate, and cooperation in mission.[3] The very name of the committee, then, immediately and (I think) rightly implies a close relationship between the concerns of the Committee on Faith and Order and of what is now the Council of Bishops Office of Christian Unity and Interreligious Relationships. And it symbolizes a long-standing United Methodist commitment to do our theological thinking, including our thinking about the nature and mission of the church, within an ecumenical context.

These shared concerns also help to explain why the committee undertook, as one of its first tasks, a major effort to articulate a theological understanding of the church: a United Methodist ecclesiology. Theologians and leaders from many branches of Methodism and beyond have wondered for a long time whether there is such a thing as a Methodist doctrine of the church. The majority opinion over the years would appear to be no, though there is also a general recognition that Methodists have a number of ecclesiological commitments, implicit if not explicit. The task given to the committee was to bring these commitments to the surface, reflect on them in the light of current needs and possibilities, and articulate a coherent United Methodist understanding of the church for these times.

As the committee was getting underway with its study, the

---

3   Michael Kinnamon, "What Can the Churches Say Together about the Church?" *Ecclesiology 8* (2012): 296, reprinted in his *Can a Renewal Movement Be Renewed?* (Grand Rapids, MI: Wm. B. Eerdmans Publishing Company, 2014), where the passage referred to is on page 40; the internal quotation is from *The Nature and Mission of the Church*, Faith and Order Paper 198 (Geneva: World Council of Churches, 2005), §32.

Faith and Order Commission of the World Council of Churches was bringing to completion its own long-awaited "convergence text" on the doctrine of the church under the title *The Church: Towards a Common Vision*.[4] This meant that the United Methodist committee's work on the topic could take advantage of that achievement, and proceed in conversation with this new ecumenical document. Since members of several Methodist churches across the world had been heavily involved in the production of the World Council of Churches statement, connections were not difficult to find, and those connections have influenced both the structure and the content of the present study document.

As readers of these pages will recognize, the title "Wonder, Love, and Praise" is derived from a line of the Charles Wesley hymn "Love Divine, All Loves Excelling":

> Finish, then, thy new creation;
> pure and spotless let us be.
> Let us see thy great salvation
> perfectly restored in thee;
> changed from glory into glory,
> till in heaven we take our place,
> till we cast our crowns before thee,
> lost in wonder, love, and praise.[5]

Wesley appears to have borrowed that line "lost in wonder, love, and praise" from a hymn by his contemporary, the English

---

4   Faith and Order Paper No. 214 (Geneva: World Council of Churches, 2014), downloadable at http://www.oikoumene.org/en/resources/documents/wcc-commissions/faith-and-order-commission/i-unity-the-church-and-its-mission/the-church-towards-a-common-vision. It is also available there in several other languages.

5   *The United Methodist Hymnal* (Nashville: The United Methodist Publishing House, 1989), no. 384.

poet and essayist Joseph Addison.[6] *Wonder, Love, and Praise* is also the title of a supplemental hymnal published by the Episcopal Church in the United States some twenty years ago,[7] and the phrase has occurred in the titles of a number of other works over the years, as one might expect. What particularly commends it in this case, however, is the way it represents a Wesleyan, Trinitarian understanding of what life is all about. In another hymn, Charles Wesley writes that we human creatures are called to be "transcripts of the Trinity."[8] By a kind of creaturely participation in the life of the triune God, we are meant for wonder, love, and praise. As John Wesley put it in one of his sermons, human beings are "created in the image of God, and designed to know, to love, and to enjoy [their] Creator to all eternity."[9] That is our chief end. That is the calling, the vocation, that Jesus Christ reveals to us, and that the Holy Spirit empowers us to accept.[10] And this is the reality of which the church is to be the sign and servant.

The study document has a three-part structure. In the first part, it identifies some Wesleyan or Methodist presuppositions for a doctrine of the church. It speaks there of three distinctive convictions that shape United Methodist thinking on the church. Then in the second part these three convictions are related to three key themes in the ecumenical document, *The Church: Towards a Common Vision*, bringing our particular

---

6   "When all thy mercies, O my God, / my rising soul surveys, / transported with the view, I'm lost / in wonder, love and praise." Joseph Addison, "Hymn on Gratitude to the Deity," in *The poetical works of the Right Honourable Joseph Addison, Esq.* (Glasgo: np, 1750), 198.

7   *Wonder, Love, and Praise: A Supplement to the Hymnal 1982* (New York: Church Publishing, 1997).

8   "Sinners, Turn: Why Will You Die," *The United Methodist Hymnal* (Nashville: The United Methodist Publishing House, 1989), no. 346.

9   John Wesley, "God's Approbation of His Works," in *Sermons II*, ed. Albert C. Outler, vol. 2 of *The Bicentennial Edition of the Works of John Wesley* (Nashville: Abingdon Press, 1985), 397.

10 Charles M. Wood, "Methodist Doctrine: An Understanding," in *Love That Rejoices in the Truth: Theological Explorations* (Eugene, OR: Cascade Books, 2009), 1–22.

heritage as United Methodists into conversation with the wider ecumenical discussion. These two parts essentially lay out the vision of the church that is being proposed to us. The third part takes up three questions having to do with our current and future practice as a church that arise from this exploration.

1.

The three distinctive convictions identified in the first part are that the saving love of God is meant for all people, not just for a favored few; that it is a transformative love; and that it is a community-creating love. To amplify a bit, quoting from the document (lines 158–206):

> *The saving love of God is meant for all people*: "God our Savior . . . desires everyone to be saved and to come to the knowledge of the truth" (1 Timothy 2:4). John Wesley's comment on this statement in his *Explanatory Notes upon the New Testament* emphasizes the "everyone": *all* of humankind is included in this desire—"Not a part only, much less the smallest part." He also notes another implication of the statement: "They are not compelled."[11] The grace of God extended to all does not override human freedom, but activates it, so that our salvation, while entirely a gift, involves our free participation. These two points about the universality of God's saving love are repeated throughout his writing and embodied in his ministry. They were essential to Wesley's understanding of the gospel, and to the power of the movement he inspired. They remain a vital part of United Methodist affirmation.

---

11 John Wesley, *Explanatory Notes upon the New Testament* (London: The Epworth Press, 1950), 775.

The love of God is transformative: To use the language familiar to Wesley and his contemporaries, as God's grace is accepted in faith, it brings both "justification," the restoration of a right relationship with God, and "sanctification," the renewal of our very being. There is a new birth. The love of God *for* us becomes the love of God *in* us. In the words of the apostle Paul, "For freedom Christ has set us free" (Galatians 5:1), and being "called to freedom," we are to "live by the Spirit," which means living by the love of God that empowers us to put aside "the works of the flesh" and to bear "the fruit of the Spirit . . . love, joy, peace, patience, kindness, generosity, faithfulness, gentleness, and self-control" (Galatians 5:13,16,19, 22). A hallmark of John Wesley's preaching, and of the preaching and testimony of the people called Methodist through the years, is that such an experienced, here-and-now transformation of human life by the power of the Holy Spirit is real.

The love of God creates community: The transformation just described is by its very nature a transformation of our relationships with others. It is through others that we experience the love of God; it is with others that the pattern of new life that God gives is both learned and lived out. . . . The church exists because the Spirit of God leads us into community, perhaps with persons with whom we would least expect to associate. . . . Wesley and those in connection with him found themselves moving beyond the established norms of churchly behavior, and challenging the church, by their own example, to enact more fully God's gift of community. Thus the term "connection" took on new resonances of meaning, as what Wesley called "social holiness"—the growth in love and in the other fruits of the Spirit that is possible only in community—was realized in new situations and settings. . . .

Together, these convictions shape our United Methodist understanding of what it is to be the church. The ways they have come to expression in our history account in part for our particular ways of being the church, within the larger Body of Christ.

The story of their coming to expression has been, as the paper notes, "a complex and often ambiguous history of accomplishments and failures, growth and loss, separations and unions, over the past two centuries and more—a very human history, in which (as its participants would want to testify) God has been steadily at work both within and despite human plans, decisions, and actions" (lines 258–61). *Wonder, Love, and Praise* offers a brief sketch of some of our denominational history and our ecumenical efforts in illustrating this point. It is extremely important, if we are to have any worthwhile theological understanding of the church, that we recognize that ambiguity; that we acknowledge, for example, the racism, nationalism, and cultural captivity that have characterized our journey, as well as the ways we have been led and empowered at times to resist and overcome them.

2.

In the second part of the paper, these three convictions are related to three themes in the recent convergence text from the World Council of Churches, *The Church: Towards a Common Vision*. Here they are taken in a different order, beginning with the affirmation that the saving love of God creates community. This reordering allows a recognition that the ecumenical text begins with the community-forming power of the love of God, relating this directly to the mission of the church. The first paragraph of its first chapter, entitled "God's Mission and the Unity of the Church," affirms:

> The Church, as the body of Christ, acts by the power of the Holy Spirit to continue his life-giving mission in prophetic and compassionate ministry and so participates in God's work of healing a broken world. Communion, whose source is the very life of the Holy Trinity, is both the gift by which the Church lives and, at the same time, the gift that God calls the church to offer to a wounded and divided humanity in hope of reconciliation and healing (1, page 5).

Citing the "Great Commission" of Matthew 28:18-20, it goes on to comment:

> This command by Jesus already hints at what he wanted his Church to be in order to carry out this mission. It was to be a community of witness, proclaiming the kingdom which Jesus had first proclaimed, inviting human beings from all nations to saving faith. It was to be a community of worship, initiating new members by baptism in the name of the Holy Trinity. It was to be a community of discipleship, in which the apostles, by proclaiming the Word, baptizing and celebrating the Lord's Supper, were to guide new believers to observe all that Jesus himself had commanded.

Methodists can relate to all this, as our own document attests with some reference to John Wesley's teachings, to Charles Wesley's hymns, and to our common liturgy for Holy Communion.

Our study text moves on, secondly (lines 445ff.), to the conviction that the saving love of God is meant for all. This leads to a brief summary, informed by the ecumenical discussion, of different senses and definitions of "church," and to an exploration of different ways in which people might be said to be participating in the *koinonia*, the communion, that the Spirit is creating. It leads to such an exploration because we might well wonder, as John Wesley did: If God wills all to be saved, then "why [is] Christianity . . . not spread as far as sin?"[12]

A distinction that may well come to have a more prominent role in future thinking about the church is used here. It is a distinction not between two churches but between two *aspects* of the church: the church as the *community of salvation* and the church as the *community of witness*. The church as we know it is called to be both: to be both a community in which persons are coming to fullness of life and a community with a mission to be Christ's witnesses in the world.

But, like John Wesley, we in The United Methodist Church have no reason to believe or teach that God's saving grace cannot reach beyond the churches that we know. The study text works with that distinction, then, to suggest that there may be an "ecclesial" aspect to the life of persons who are outside what is sometimes called the "visible" church who are responding positively to God's grace. It is "ecclesial" in the sense that they are being drawn into communion with God and with their fellow creatures, as the grace of God is inherently community forming, even though they may not (or not yet) be part of the explicit community of witness. This possibility has implications for (among other things) how we who call ourselves Christian might regard our non-Christian neighbors and the religious traditions and communities to which many of them belong. And it might help us gain some clarity about our own particular mission as the "visible" church: to be a sign and servant of the triune God's redeeming, community-creating

---

12 Wesley, "The Imperfection of Human Knowledge," *Works*, 2:581.

work in the world. What this means for our practice depends on the particular circumstances in which we find ourselves, and this of course varies considerably from place to place.

What guides us as we pursue that mission? That question brings us to the third of the distinctive Wesleyan convictions enunciated earlier in the text—that the saving love of God is transformative—and to its counterpart in the ecumenical document's treatment of the way in which the church is to serve as a sign and servant of God's work of restoring human beings to their vocation. Not surprisingly, this has something to do with faith, hope, and love. One way of approaching this—a very Wesleyan way—is through the traditional theme of the "threefold office" of Christ, the three dimensions or aspects of his saving work: in traditional language, as prophet, priest, and king. The prophetic office has to do with his bringing us to know the truth; the priestly office has to do with his healing our relationship with God; and the kingly or royal office has to do with his guiding and empowering us toward fullness of life in community. The church, through its proclamation of the Word, its celebration of the sacraments, and the ordering of its common life, bears witness to what God has done and is doing through Jesus Christ and in the power of the Holy Spirit. It is in this way that our Articles of Religion and Confession of Faith affirm the classic Reformation definitions of the visible church of Christ—and also find much common ground with other streams of Christian tradition so that together we might understand the church to be "a community of witness, . . . a community of worship, . . . [and] a community of discipleship" (lines 652ff.).

Wonder, Love, and Praise calls us to acknowledge in this connection that (borrowing the words of the Westminster Confession) "this visible church hath been sometimes more, sometimes less visible" (lines 569ff.). The visibility at stake here has little to do with the amount of real estate a particular church owns, the size of its membership roll or its budget, or the impressiveness of its architecture. It has to do rather with the extent to which this particular community in its particular circumstances is showing forth the love that rejoices in the truth (1 Corinthians 13:6): that is, the extent to which it is truly the community of witness, worship, and discipleship that it claims to be.

There are other themes taken up in this second part of the document that I must pass over in this brief review. There are, for example, some elements for a basic theology of ministry and ministerial leadership. There is also some reflection on the ecumenical document's helpful treatment of diversity in the church—"Legitimate diversity in the life of communion is a gift from the Lord," which the document affirms (28, page 16)—as well on some of our struggles with that gift (lines 599ff.). While more on this aspect appears below, this review of the first two parts of Wonder, Love, and Praise closes by returning briefly to the theme of ambiguity that I mentioned earlier.

In a recent and well-received book on ecclesiology entitled Church, World and the Christian Life, Nicholas M. Healy laments the fact that so many proposed theological understandings of the church are what he calls "blueprint ecclesiologies."[13] They look very attractive on paper but they do not adequately take into account the situation on the ground. I am reminded of Francis Bacon's line, written some four hundred years ago, about "philosophers" who "make imaginary laws for imaginary commonwealths; and their discourses are as the stars, which give little light because they are so high."[14] We could easily find ourselves with a blueprint ecclesiology

---

13 Nicholas M. Healy, *Church, World, and Christian Life: Practical-Prophetic Ecclesiology* (Cambridge: Cambridge University Press, 2000), 32–49 passim.
14 Quoted in L. C. Knights, Explorations (New York: New York University Press, 1964), 115.

if we just rested content with the affirmation that the church is the gift of God, and implicitly denied, or at least neglected to attend to, the fact that it is also our creation. As we receive the gift, as we appropriate it—to *appropriate* something means "to make something one's own"—we shape it to our own uses, as well as shaping ourselves in accord with it. *We make use of the church* in all sorts of ways; and these human uses deserve our careful study and reflection. As our text says (lines 416–26):

> Like other religious traditions and communities, Christian churches serve a variety of human needs and purposes, in ways that vary a great deal from one place and time to another. They commonly serve human needs for order, coherence, stability, belief-reinforcement, companionship, ethical guidance, and so forth. They are affected at every point by the typical ways human beings interact with each other in the satisfaction of those needs. They are also put to use in the service of other interests on the part of adherents and "outsiders" alike, for example, by being made to serve particular political and economic ends. No one acquainted with the history of the Christian churches from the earliest centuries onward can fail to acknowledge this complex intertwining of human needs, desires, ambitions, and fears in that history. Sometimes it is much easier to recognize those elements in the life of the church in some other place and time than in one's own.

This ambiguity, so evident in our own history and current experience, is well described by another recent writer who observes that the church is a divine-human institution. The Spirit is mixed up in it, and we do not know what it looks like until it is already before us. Nobody invented the . . . church, nor would anybody have invented it in the form in which it evolved. It could not have emerged without builders, of course, for which reason there was and is much that is human about it, sometimes for good, sometimes not. But the Lord also builds the house.[15]

The church is the gift of the triune God. It is inherent in the gift of saving grace, the grace that is offered to all, that draws us into community with the triune God and with other human creatures, and that, in doing so, transforms our lives so that we may learn to live in love, truth, and joy and thanksgiving. To be disciples is to be learners, after all; that is the very meaning of the word. As disciples of Jesus Christ, who is "the way, the truth, and the life," we are called and empowered to recover our human vocation to live in wonder, love, and praise, and, by so doing, to bear witness to that possibility to others: to help others also to become learners, to accept his yoke and learn from him. In this way the church is both a school of wisdom and a community of witness.

But in affirming this, we must also keep in mind the implications of the fact that "the Church is both a divine and a human reality." It is *God's gift* to us, but it is God's gift *to us*, and we have the freedom and the responsibility that comes with being recipients of such a gift.

3.

The third and final part of *Wonder, Love, and Praise* deals with some questions that I take to be relevant to reflection on the issues before us here and now.

---

15 Paul Valliere, *Conciliarism: A History of Decision-Making in the Church* (Cambridge: Cambridge University Press, 2012), 69.

First, how might we characterize the particular role of The United Methodist Church within the "Church Universal"? What is its niche in the ecclesial ecology? Second, what insights might our participation in the ecumenical discussion generate to help us deal more constructively and effectively with the vexing issues surrounding "legitimate diversity," both as they affect our own life and mission in The United Methodist Church and in our ongoing relations with other Christian communities? Third, how might a renewed ecclesial vision inform our deliberations about our polity—that is, about how we structure our common life in the service of our mission?

Regarding the first question, the paper proposes three markers of United Methodist identity. These are not exclusive to our tradition, and the extent to which we actually succeed in living them out is, of course, another question, but these would seem to be things we would like to be known by. One (lines 849ff.) has to do with the scope of grace, in both senses of the term *scope*: that is, the *extent* of God's grace (offered to all, not just to a privileged few), and its *aim*, or what it is meant to accomplish (our full renewal in God's image, what the Gospel of John calls "fullness of life" for all of God's creatures). The vision of the church proposed in the first two parts of the paper is certainly in accord with this marker.

A second marker of United Methodist identity (lines 890ff.) has to do with the characteristic both of polity and of ethos that we associate with the term *connectionalism*, which is addressed in more detail below.

The third marker named is (lines 911ff.)

a commitment to *theological reflection* as the task of the whole church. The presence in the *Book of*

Discipline not only of doctrinal standards, but also of a statement on "our theological task," indicates the importance of this commitment. Note that theological reflection does not *replace* standards of doctrine; we need and affirm both.

"The theological task," the Discipline says, "though related to the Church's doctrinal expressions, serves a different function. Our doctrinal affirmations assist us in the discernment of Christian truth in ever-changing contexts. Our theological task includes the testing, renewal, elaboration, and application of our doctrinal perspective in carrying out our calling 'to spread scriptural holiness over these lands.'"[16]

By their very character and content, our doctrinal standards not only permit but require the sort of responsible, thoughtful critical engagement that "Our Theological Task" describes. Our theological work must be "both critical and constructive," "both individual and communal," "contextual and incarnational," and "essentially practical."[17]

This sort of theological work belongs to every responsible body and responsible individual in the church.

On the second of our questions, "What insights might our participation in the ecumenical discussion generate to help us deal more constructively and effectively with the vexing issues surrounding 'legitimate diversity,' both as they affect our own life and mission in The United Methodist Church and in our ongoing relations with other Christian communities?" here is a pertinent passage from the study text (lines 935-46):

---

16   *Book of Discipline 2012,* ¶105:78). [Citation in original.]
17   *Book of Discipline 2012,* ¶105: 79-80). [Citation in original.]

It should be said that our problem is not conflict. Our problem is in the way we sometimes deal with conflict. We would do well to remember at the outset that conflict is a "given" in the church. It is to be expected. Disagreements creating conflict may arise over (to use the Wesleyan language) "what to teach, how to teach, and what to do."[18] Embedded in and accompanying these disagreements may be other, sometimes hidden or unacknowledged, difficulties also leading to tensions: antagonisms stemming from the complex histories and relationships of the persons and groups involved, differences over political or cultural values, struggles over the possession and uses of power, and so forth. Different sources and varieties of conflict may be interrelated In any given Instance. Given the variety of the human uses of the church, it sometimes happens that conflict over one issue is promoted or exploited by individuals or groups as a means of accomplishing some other aim, or in order to satisfy other needs. Conflict is as complex as it is common.

The paper goes on to say that our having differing judgments among us on important matters may be a good and productive thing, if it leads us into sharing our experiences and insights in ways that yield new understanding—understanding that surpasses whatever any one of us may have brought into the conversation. In this way, difference is a value, and we ought not to put a premium on the avoidance of conflict. We ought, instead, to show the world how conflict can be explored thoughtfully and in an atmosphere of

---

18 *The Methodist Societies: The Minutes of Conference*, ed. Henry D. Rack, vol. 10, *The Bicentennial Edition of the Works of John Wesley* (Nashville: Abingdon Press, 2011), 778.

mutual respect, as an occasion for growth. The English Roman Catholic theologian Nicholas Lash tells of a parish priest who one day remarked of a neighboring parish, "They have so little charity in that place that they can't even disagree with each other."[19] Woe to the church of which that can be said, whether it is a local congregation or a denomination.

Especially relevant to the situation of a church that has moved into many different cultures and contexts—such as Nicholas Lash's, or our own—is the fact that, as our study document says (lines 961ff.),

> some differences within the church aid the church in its mission to a diverse world. New technologies give rise to previously unimagined possibilities; new knowledge changes our understanding of ourselves and of the world in which we live. When the church is confronted with a new situation and is pondering its best response, it is well to have a wide range of experience and perspectives at hand. To understand and respect one another's differences and the ways in which they contribute to the church's fulfillment of its mission is itself a mode of sharing; and something like the ecumenical pattern of "convergence," in which differences are held in the midst of a deeper and richer unity, is a hoped-for experience.

When we are faced with unavoidable differences that appear to threaten that deeper and richer unity, however—when we seem to have a situation on our hands that goes beyond "legitimate diversity"—what then? At that point, our study document first says (lines 987–92): not so fast.

---

19 Nicholas Lash, "The Church—A School of Wisdom?" in *Receptive Ecumenism and the Call to Catholic Learning*, ed. Paul D. Murray (Oxford: Oxford University Press, 2008), 72.

One important consideration in this connection is that we may not yet be in a position to render a responsible judgment on the matter at hand. We may not know all that we need to know. We may not have adequate conceptual resources. We may not have the spiritual maturity to see what we need to see. We may not even have posed our questions rightly. We may, in short, need to gain some intellectual and emotional humility, and to cultivate some dispositions that would permit wisdom to grow.

We may also be succumbing to a very human tendency to block and reject the very things we need. Ruled knowingly or unknowingly by our fears or our self-interests, we may instead pursue strategies that will subvert mutual understanding and create deeper separation, even alienation. In this connection our paper turns to some familiar counsel of John Wesley's, from his sermon on "Catholic Spirit" and from his introduction to his published *Standard Sermons* (lines 993–1035). But such counsel is only effective when it is received and taken to heart. Maybe we need to take a further step.

The Wesleyan counsel quoted in the study paper—such as his observation that we can be sure that we are mistaken in at least part of what we take to be true, but we may not know in just *which* part—came to Wesley, directly or indirectly, from some seventeenth-century English Protestant writers. Some of their wisdom was compiled and published for the benefit of the Methodists in America by Bishop Francis Asbury in 1792, under the title *The Causes, Evils, and Cures of Heart and Church Divisions*.[20] It was composed of selections from

---

20 Francis Asbury, *The Causes, Evils, and Cures, of Heart and Church Divisions: Extracted from the Works of Mr. Richard Baxter, and Mr. Jeremiah Burroughs* (Philadelphia: Printed by Parry Hall, 1792). The book was frequently reprinted in the nineteenth century and has lately been reproduced electronically and in print. An abridged paraphrase "study edition" was offered by Abingdon Press in 2016, prior to the General Conference.

the works of two Puritan leaders, Jeremiah Burroughs and Richard Baxter. They, along with a number of their colleagues both in Britain and in North America, had something to do with the eventual development of what we have come to call "denominations." For these seventeenth-century leaders, as they were contemplating separating (or being separated) from the established Church of England, it was vital to recognize that one's own church is part of the church universal, but not the whole church, and that the scope of the true church is known only to God. They believed that they were right to act upon their own convictions, yet importantly, "they were aware that they might be wrong."[21] And so, rather than regarding all other churches as false and schismatic, they avowed a hope to learn from them. As one such group wrote to those from whom they had recently parted: "We see as much cause to suspect the integrity of our own hearts as yours; and so much the more, as being more privy to the deceitfulness of our own hearts than to yours . . . which causeth us with great reverence to accept and receive what further light God may be pleased to impart to us by you."[22]

These leaders believed that differences among Christians may, in fact, may be used by God to bring us to a fuller understanding of the truth. One historian describing these developments rightly and vitally observed: "This, quite obviously, is no doctrine of relativity so far as truth itself is concerned; the relativity is in terms of one's apprehension of the truth."[23] To apply such insights to how we deal not only with differences among the churches but also with differences within our own church community may be among our most pressing tasks.

---

21 Winthrop S. Hudson, "Denominationalism as a Basis for Ecumenicity: A Seventeenth Century Conception," *Church History 24* (1955): 36.
22 *An Apologetical Narration* (1643), quoted in Hudson, "Denominationalism as a Basis," 35.
23 Hudson, "Denominationalism as a Basis," 40.

This leads us naturally into the third of the questions raised in the final part of the study paper: How might a renewed ecclesial vision inform our deliberations about our polity—that is, about how we structure our common life in the service of our mission? *Wonder, Love, and Praise* (lines 1056ff.) observes:

> [A church's polity] has to do with the way the church orders its own life responsibly so as to fulfill its calling. . . . The way the church orders its own life is itself an aspect of its witness to the world. When its polity enables and manifests an openness to the community-forming power of the Holy Spirit, when it serves the church's mandate "to maintain the unity of the Spirit in the bond of peace" (Ephesians 4:3) with such power and clarity as to bring to humankind a new understanding of the possibilities for fruitful life together, then it has fulfilled its purpose.

As United Methodists, "we need forms of polity that are consistent with our core convictions: that is, forms that honor the radically inclusive scope of God's saving grace, forms that recognize and build upon the transformative character of that grace, and forms that will serve, rather than subvert, the growth of genuine community" (lines 1091–95).

That is quite an order. In its brief comment on this question (lines 1095ff.), *Wonder, Love, and Praise* refers to the Methodist usage of "conference" as a resource. It may be well to bring into the picture the other hallowed Wesleyan concept that was mentioned earlier, that of *connectionalism*—if only for a moment. One problem is that there is no concept of connectionalism; or perhaps more accurately, there are many concepts of it.[24] Methodist use of the term *connexion* arose in the eighteenth century and derived from the fact that certain religious societies in Britain were at that time considered legitimate or lawful if they were supervised by, or "in connexion with," an Anglican cleric. As John Wesley was a bona fide Anglican cleric, the Methodist societies were set up to be in connection with him; and he insisted on this point, vigorously. As anyone familiar with John Wesley's leadership style might attest, *connection* in his day did not immediately have some of the connotations we have come to associate with it, of interdependence, mutuality, consultation, the sharing of power, and so forth. It chiefly meant being under Wesley's direction, or under the direction of those appointed by him. It had, and for many it still has, strong connotations of centralized authority, and of an effective chain of command. These can be in some tension with the other connotations just mentioned, though it should be granted that tension goes with just about any arrangement involving authority.

Wonder, Love, and Praise suggests that "'conciliarity' is a related (though not synonymous) term in the ecumenical discussion" for what connectionalism has come to mean among us. That is not a novel idea. A number of ecumenical theologians—not only Methodists—have recognized a kinship between the way Methodists have come to speak of connection (as a "network of relationships") and conciliar thought.[25] Conciliarity has to do with the ways that local Christian churches, or groups of them, relate to each other either directly or through representative gatherings to learn from each other and occasionally to decide on matters of common concern,

---

24 Russell M. Richey has devoted much effort to sorting out this subject. See, for example, his *Methodist Connectionalism: Historical Perspectives* (Nashville: General Board of Higher Education and Ministry, 2009).

25 See, e.g., Valliere, *Conciliarism*, 10, 30.

on which it is deemed important for them to have a common witness or practice. The Methodist conference system, understood as a connectional system, can be seen as a form of conciliarity. But "conciliarity" in its fuller usage is a term that might move both "conference" and "connectionalism" in a promising direction, if we were to explore it further. It may help to undergird those related values of interdependence, mutuality, consultation, and sharing of power, and might help us understand better how we might embed such values in our polity. A conciliar model might be a fruitful guide to our future as a worldwide church, enriching our current repertoire of concepts. That is to say, conciliarity has implications internally, with regard to our polity and relationships within The United Methodist Church, as well as externally, with regard to our relationships with other Christian communities.

It may be particularly important to undertake this exploration now, as The United Methodist Church seeks guidance for its own internal life as well as for its relations with other Christian bodies. The report of the Task Group on the Global Nature of The United Methodist Church to the 2008 General Conference expressed a hope that as we embrace that global or (as we would say now) wordwide nature, we might "model a new way of being church in the world" and "offer the world a better version of unity and interdependence."[26] And it offered this critique of the current structure of the church: "It disempowers central conferences from being fully actualized within the body and allows the church in the United States to escape responsibility from dealing with

---

26 "Worldwide Ministry through The United Methodist Church: A Report of the Task Group on the Global Nature of the Church," *Daily Christian Advocate, Advance Edition* (2008): 945. On first reading I thought that "version" was probably a misprint for "vision." But perhaps what was meant was indeed "a better version of unity and interdependence," better, that is, than the version(s) offered by schemes for economic globalization.

its internal issues." Both the hope and the critique might be constructively addressed by going more deeply into the promise of conciliarity.

The United Methodist Church recognizes itself as a denomination, as did its predecessor bodies pretty much from the time they got organized as churches. Historians and sociologists who study such things are generally agreed that although its roots may go back through English Protestantism to the Reformation, the denomination as a "way of being church" is largely an American product, fitted to American circumstances. Not all churches even within the United States readily fit the description of a denomination: Catholics and Episcopalians, long regarding themselves as parts of a worldwide communion and structure, have difficulty matching their experience and self-understanding to that model, though they may admit that for practical purposes within a given national or regional setting they have to fit themselves partly into that frame; many Baptists have strong reservations about the idea, believing that the congregation is the real church; and at the same time a fair number of mega-churches, independent missions, nondenominational movements, and other sorts of Christian enterprises reject the model. Sometimes such movements *become* denominations in fact, if not in self-understanding, as their needs for stability, organization, authorized leadership and so on reach a certain point within civil contexts where "denomination" is the expected form of religious organization.

At their best, denominations are ways of giving the Christian movement the structure and resources it needs to thrive. There is an increasing recognition, though still a contested one, that "denomination" can be a useful category in ecclesiology. It can play a proper role in our theological understanding of the church—or at least, one that we cannot safely ignore—as an "intermediary" form of church. One student of the form has written that "denominations exist to mediate between two realities: the church universal and the local congregation. Denominations exist rightly only when they serve as a means for something else. . . . It is idolatry for denominations to proclaim themselves to be ends, whether the proclamation is made in word or deed."[27] Still, whether the denomination is the most apt conceptual category for envisioning our particular future is an open question.

A question that has come in for some discussion lately is whether, or to what extent, the denomination is a serviceable institutional form in a worldwide context. The burden of proof would appear to fall on those who would want to give an affirmative answer. As noted, Anglicans and Catholics, who see themselves as members of worldwide communions, would not apply the term to themselves In that context at least, if at all. Nor would the Orthodox churches. Lutheran, Reformed, and free-church Protestant traditions, though generally organized as denominations or something close to that in many national or regional contexts, are not worldwide denominations. We have instead the Presbyterian Church in the United States; the Evangelical Church in Germany (itself composed of some twenty regional bodies); the Lutheran Church in Liberia; and so forth. The Lutheran World Federation and the World Communion of Reformed Churches are not striving for organic unity as one institution, but rather for something like conciliar fellowship. And indeed—as Michael Kinnamon's list of "tangible signs of the new life of communion" would indicate—something like conciliar fellowship has come to replace the old ideal of organic union as the goal of the ecumenical movement overall, as churches have reflected together on "the nature of the unity we seek."

---

27 Barry Ensign-George, "Denomination as Ecclesiological Category: Sketching an Assessment," in *Denomination: Assessing an Ecclesiological Category*, ed. Paul M. Collins and Barry Ensign-George (London: T. & T. Clark International, 2011), 6.

If we look back on the past forty or more years of efforts by The United Methodist Church and its predecessors to come up with a structure more in keeping with the fact that this "denomination" resides in many countries on several continents and under vastly different social, cultural, political, and economic conditions, we may wonder to what extent these repeated efforts have come to grief because they have assumed, and even insisted upon, a denominational model for the "world church."[28] Indeed, I might ask in my relative ignorance (if not total innocence) to what extent the results have been determined by the effects of denominational*ism*—that is, the kind of idolatry in which the denomination becomes the end rather than the means. This is, as I say, a question raised in ignorance. However, I might ask more constructively to what extent other models than the denomination have been seriously entertained in these deliberations. How much thought has been given to how thorough a recasting of the denominational model would be required in order to make it work? Denominations are in trouble, in their traditional forms and functions, in many places in the world, for many reasons. It may be that we need something quite different for our future. And it may be that we have untapped resources within our United Methodist traditions as well as in the broader Christian tradition to bring to bear on this need.

In recent years the Roman Catholic Church has described itself as a "community of communities." In this spirit, a group of Lutheran and Catholic theologians meeting together for several years to work on the issues separating the churches has

---

28 For an overview up to 1998, see R. Lawrence Turnipseed, "A Brief History of the Discussion of The United Methodist Church as a 'World Church,'" in *The Ecumenical Implications of the Discussions of "The Global Nature of The United Methodist Church,"* ed. Bruce Robbins (New York: General Commission on Christian Unity and Interreligious Concerns, 1999), 12–34. A similar account and analysis of the past two decades might be instructive.

proposed thinking of the church universal as a community or communion of churches (*communio ecclesiarum, Gemeinschaft der Kirchen*).[29] A leading Orthodox theologian some years ago remarked that "before we understand the place and the function of the council *in* the church, we must . . . see *the Church itself as a council.*"[30] With such images before it, the World Council of Churches some years ago observed: "As the church itself is an 'assembly' and appears as assembly both in worship and many other expressions of its life, so it needs both at the local and on all other possible levels representative assemblies in order to answer the questions which it faces."[31] Each of these ways of speaking of a noncentralized unity in diversity, or diversity in unity, has a particular resonance and transmits particular values; perhaps the most straightforward for our purposes would be simply to envision the church as a community of communities.

We have been urged repeatedly in recent years to "rethink church," and to find "a new way of being church." To do so in our present moment requires moving beyond a US-centric denominational self-understanding, and moving beyond some of the temptations of denominationalism that may arise in connection with a national or cultural identity, toward greater catholicity—a catholicity *ad intra* as well as *ad extra*, so to speak. This in turn requires holding fast to some of the key insights of those English Puritan forebears mentioned earlier: that we—any particular "we"—are not the whole church, that we might be wrong in some of our convictions, and that we need to listen closely to those with

29 Group of Farfa Sabina, *Communion of Churches and Petrine Ministry: Lutheran-Catholic Convergences*, trans. Paul Misner (Grand Rapids, MI: Eerdmans, 2014).

30 Alexander Schmemann, "Towards a Theology of Councils," *Church, World, Mission: Reflections on Orthodoxy in the West* (Crestwood, NY: St. Vladimir's Seminary Press, 1979), 163.

31 *Councils and the Ecumenical Movement*, World Council of Churches Studies 5 (Geneva: World Council of Churches, 1968), 10.

whom we differ in order to hear whatever God may be saying to us through them.

The question for The United Methodist Church at this juncture is a local parallel to the question that drives the ecumenical discussion: How are we to find and live out an adequately diversified form of Christian community—one that could be a model and inspiration for an adequately diversified *human* community?

Ted Campbell, in an address to the World Methodist Council in September 2016, said that the question before United Methodists now may not be whether we divide—he suggested that division is fairly likely, if not inevitable—but rather "whether we can divide well, or as well as possible. Are there ways for Methodist church bodies to divide that will minimize the distractions to mission that so often accompany divisions? That will allow more easily for future unities? That will perhaps create new unities even at the points of division? Can we divide in ways that keep us somehow responsible to our Wesleyan and ecumenical partners?"[32] I appreciate his way of putting the question. I also appreciate his saying, earlier in the address, that if what we are faced with is a separation into two groups, he would have a hard time fitting into either one. I am right there with him. United Methodists are really not divisible into two groups. (James Thurber says somewhere, "People can be divided into two groups. There are those who divide people into two groups, and there are those who don't." I belong to the second group.)[33] So my question is this: Can we, by the grace of God, come up with a way to allow adequate diversification that does not involve division, and that, over time, permits a fuller realization of

---

32 Ted A. Campbell, "One Faith: Address to World Methodist Conference, September 1, 2016," unpublished. I am grateful to Professor Campbell for a copy of his address.

33 See Charles M. Wood, "The Primacy of Scripture," *Love That Rejoices in the Truth: Theological Explorations* (Eugene, OR: Cascade Books, 2009), 35–42.

and witness to genuine unity?

As noted earlier, there are times when we human beings are not at all interested in seeking or promoting mutual understanding. Sometimes we will do our best to avoid or prevent it. We have a range of effective instruments at hand for that purpose. Fear is one of the more accessible and more potent of these. When, for instance, we find that someone is trying to make us afraid, it is well to try to discover why they are doing so, and what they have to gain by our fear. Often, what they will gain—or at least what they hope to gain—is some sort of power or control. Our fear may cause us to stop doing something we are doing, something the fear-mongers do not want done. Or it may cause us to become suspicious of someone else, or to become defensive rather than open in our relations with others, and all of this may work to someone else's perceived advantage. The use of "wedge issues" and polarizing strategies in the churches as well as in our civil communities has become all too common, and it is up to all of us to see this for what it is, and to resist it: to refuse to divide people into two groups, and to insist on finding ways to make our conflicts serve our mission.

There are four ecclesiological concepts that might be of use to us here, if only as examples of the sort of imagination we may need. One is *subsidiarity*; another is *reconciled diversity*; the third is *differentiated consensus*; and the fourth is *reception*.

Subsidiarity is perhaps the simplest to employ, in principle. As commonly stated, it is the principle that decisions are to be made and policies adopted on the lowest possible level. The language of "levels" may be unfortunate, but it seems built into the term itself. Instead of "on the lowest possible level" we might say "in the least general, or most specific, context allowable." Perhaps we need a term that evokes the image not of higher-ups and lower-downs, but of smaller circles within larger circles, whether we are thinking geographically or in some other relevant frame. Put another way: "This principle consists in not taking from individuals the tasks which they are able to undertake on their own, and in avoiding the transfer to a higher authority of functions that those authorities more immediately concerned can normally assume."[34] Some version of this principle is, I take it, at work in the current effort to work out a "General Book of Discipline" dealing with those things that are essential to the maintenance and flourishing of our unity as United Methodists, and then to leave it to regional conferences to work out the legislation and polity arrangements that are most suitable to their own circumstances where general uniformity is not required. If all goes well, the principle can be carried further in to smaller units including the local congregation or ministry context. It is probably better, as a rule, to begin with the specific and work out toward the general, since doing it the other way around often results in giving the impression that there is a general norm (inevitably crafted from some specific context) which might, if necessary, be adapted grudgingly to local circumstances.

One advantage to subsidiarity, as one aspect of a conciliar future, is this: People have generally found it much easier to work toward mutual understanding when the effort does not involve an internal struggle over resources and power. As Upton Sinclair once observed, it is difficult to get a person to understand something when their salary depends on their not understanding it. It is not just salary that may be at stake; it could be authority, prestige, honor, privilege, self-image— in any case, the larger the context in which something is at

---

34 Le Groupe des Dombes, *"One Teacher": Doctrinal Authority in the Church*, trans. Catherine E. Clifford (Grand Rapids, MI: Eerdmans, 2010), 148–49.

issue, the larger the stakes. When the scope is reduced, or when we are able to de-escalate things and qualify the outcome of a resolution in some important ways, this may enable folks to relax just a bit, and it may open the way to a more satisfactory outcome in the longer term.

The second concept, "reconciled diversity" is, in a way, subsidiarity after the fact. The term is used explicitly by the Community of Protestant Churches in Europe to designate the way that churches with historically conflicting ways of ordering themselves—different structures of ordained ministry and oversight, for example—can recognize each other's order as legitimate, though not binding on themselves.[35] The principle applies also to some extent to diversity in matters of official doctrine and doctrinal standards. It operates at least tacitly in many other settings than the European one where it has been explicitly invoked. More recently it has been given new currency by Pope Francis's use of it in his 2013 apostolic exhortation *Evangelii Gaudium* and on subsequent occasions. There, Francis has emphasized that unity in reconciled diversity is the work of the Holy Spirit. It does not come about because we have decided to overcome our divisions, but because God is not allowing our divisions to have the last word.

With regard to some of our differences, for example, on ethical issues, the term "reconciled diversity" may sound too final, as if we were content to "agree to disagree" and no longer to explore the questions on which we differ. "Reconciled diversity" should not be applied too readily in such cases. On

---

35 The summary and critical assessment provided by the British Methodist scholar David Carter is informative: "Unity in Reconciled Diversity: Cop-out or Rainbow Church?" *Theology* 113, no. 876 (November 2010): 411–20. See also "The Unity of the Church: Gift and Calling," the Canberra Statement of the World Council of Churches (1991), at https://www.oikoumene.org/en/resources/documents/commissions/faith-and-order/i-unity-the-church-and-its-mission/the-unity-of-the-church-gift-and-calling-the-canberra-statement.

such matters, perhaps those involved need to make it clear that it is not our *differences* that are reconciled but rather that *we* are being reconciled (by God!) *despite* our differences, and that we hope to be led to fuller understanding and to fuller life together as we continue the journey.

"Differentiated consensus" is a term coined some years ago by Harding Meyer, long-time director of the Institute for Ecumenical Research in Strasbourg, that quickly came into general use. It describes the way that churches with seemingly conflicting teachings on a given point may, through a process of discussion and sharing, come to understand that these teachings are not actually in conflict. They do this by uncovering the "fundamental intentions" or originating concerns underlying seemingly opposed doctrinal statements, and finding that these—and the resulting doctrines, properly applied—are compatible. Some seemingly intractable disagreements between Catholics and Protestants on subjects such as ordination, the sacraments, and the doctrine of justification by faith, have been transformed by this experience, as the parties come to understand what gave rise to the difference. In such cases, each party can maintain its doctrine (and not rescind it, nor adopt the other's) and be understood as affirming something the other would not need to deny.[36] When this principle is applied not only to doctrines and practices arising in different historical contexts, but also to those pertaining to different *socio-cultural* contexts, it may have greater relevance to some of our current struggles.

---

36 Having used the term in ecumenical circles since around 1980, Meyer provided his own account of its meaning in an influential essay on "Ecumenical Consensus," *Gregorianum* 77, no. 2 (1996): 213–25. He offered further reflections on its development and significance in "Der Prägung einer Formel: Ursprung und Intention," in *Einheit—aber wie? Zur Tragfähigkeit der ökumenischen Formel vom "differenzierten Konsens,"* ed. Harald Wagner (Freiburg: Herder, 2000), 36–58.

Our fourth ecclesiological concept, *reception*, has received a good deal of attention in recent ecumenical work, but it refers to a phenomenon as old as the Christian church. It is closely connected with the theme of conciliarity. Briefly put, it refers to the way in which the decisions reached in council—in a synod or assembly or gathering of representative Christian leaders—only attain their real validity as they are received, interpreted, and put into practice throughout the church. Speaking of the authority of the early ecumenical councils (for instance, Nicaea and Chalcedon), a widely respected ecumenical study group observes:

> Thus, the authority of a council does not function automatically. A certain number of conditions must be met before a conciliar gathering is considered legitimate and authoritative. Among these conditions, the phenomenon of *reception* is essential. A council can never be considered apart from the process of reception to which it gives rise, that is to say, the fact that a whole group of ecclesial communities with their bishops recognize its teaching as an expression of the apostolic faith.[37]

The importance of reception is such that—as the history of the Christian movement makes clear—a relatively minor regional council may come to be regarded as an ecumenical council if its teaching comes to be widely accepted, while "the decision of an ecumenical council may be forgotten."[38] The process of reception may take decades, or longer; in a sense, it is an ongoing and never-completed process, but

---

37   Le Groupe des Dombes, "One Teacher," 14.
38   Ibid., 112.

rather one in which the church is continually receiving, under-standing, and passing on the apostolic witness.[39]

Recent ecumenical achievements such as the World Coun-cil of Churches' texts *Baptism, Eucharist and Ministry* (1983) and *The Church: Towards a Common Vision* (2014), and the Lutheran—Roman Catholic *Joint Declaration on the Doctrine of Justification* (1999), are evidence of the importance of this continuing process of reception in an ecumenical context. Here, it underlies the principle of "differentiated consensus." But consider for a moment its possible relevance to our cur-rent differences over doctrinal and ethical teaching within The United Methodist Church. What are we to make of the fact that some of the decisions on such points made by suc-cessive General Conferences—by majority votes of varying proportions—have apparently not been "received," at least not in a positive manner, by a significant proportion of our members and clergy, annual conferences and bishops? Has the concept of reception, and current ecumenical reflection on it, any bearing on this situation? If so, does it offer any guidance as to how we might best proceed to find a way forward?

These are only a few of the insights and provocations that we might garner from our ecumenical efforts, and from the renewed vision of the church that is worked out, however provisionally, in *Wonder, Love, and Praise.* I hope that the coming period of study, reflection, and response will lead to greater understanding and to a fuller realization of our com-mon vocation as Christians.

---

39 A fine, readable treatment of the concept is William G. Rusch, *Ecumenical Reception: Its Challenge and Opportunity* (Grand Rapids, MI: Wm. B. Eerdmans Publishing Co., 2007).

Helps for Group Leaders

As group leader, your role is to facilitate the sessions and listen to the group members.

- Pray as you begin preparation. Pray for each group member by name.

- Read the corresponding session in the book before the group session. Make note of any scripture references or Bible verses that seem appropriate for discussion prior to the session. Study the scripture and refer to more than one Bible translation if that is helpful to you. What speaks to you personally? What do you think God is trying to communicate to you?

- Look ahead and select specific discussion questions you plan to cover. Please don't feel compelled to answer every question. Chose the questions that best suit your group.

- Be the first person at the session. Arrive at least five minutes early so you can welcome persons as they come in. Practice gracious hospitality.

- Greet each person by name when they arrive. This is very important.

- Make sure that your meeting space is comfortable and conducive to group conversation.

- For the best sharing, arrange the chairs in a circle. Directing the group from up front just kills discussion because it sends the wrong message.

- Begin and end on time. This shows that you honor commitments and respect other people's time.

- Make sure to introduce guests and help them feel welcome.

- If there is business, keep it short.

- When listing prayer concerns, do not gossip or get sidetracked. You want to build trust in the group and gossip will hinder that. You might also find that newsprint or a chalk or white board is helpful for writing down prayer requests or questions as they arise in group conversation.

- Create a climate of openness; encourage individuals to participate in ways that are comfortable for them. Be enthusiastic. **Remember, you set the tone for the class.**

- Some people are uncomfortable talking, so occasionally let them write their responses. If no one answers at first, don't be afraid of a little silence. Count to ten silently; then say something such as, "Would anyone like to go first?" If no one responds, venture an answer yourself. Have your answers prepared ahead of time. But don't talk too much. Your answer is only meant to model how to respond, not to dominate the discussion. Then ask for comments and other responses.

- Model openness as you share with the group. Group members will follow your example. If you only share at a surface level, everyone else will follow suit. If you want a richer discussion, you need to share at a deeper level yourself.

- Be aware, however, that it is natural for the conversation to begin at a surface level and then move to a deeper level as the session goes on. These sessions are designed to begin at a surface level and go progressively deeper.

- Draw out participants without asking them to share what they are unwilling to share. Make eye contact with someone and say something like, "How about someone else?"

- Encourage multiple responses before moving on. If you want more conversation around a response, ask something like, "Has that ever happened to anyone else?"

- If you have trouble getting responses from the group, consider giving your answer first and then just going around the circle. This lowers the anxiety of those who might feel uncomfortable. But indicate that it's ok not to answer.

- Avoid asking "Why?" or "Why do you believe that?" Instead consider asking or giving an example to illustrate the point.

- Affirm responses with comments such as, "Great," or "Thanks," or "I like that," especially if this is the first time someone has spoken during the group session.

- Steer the conversation away from argument. If you feel things heating up, say something like, "You seem to feel strongly about this."

- Give everyone a chance to talk, but keep the conversation moving. Moderate to prevent a few individuals from doing all of the talking. Please note that some people will not talk unless you call on them and some will talk all the time if you let them.

- Monitor your own contributions. If you are doing most of the talking, back off.

- Remember that you do not have to have all the answers. Your job is to keep the discussion going and encourage participation. If there are questions that need further research, just write them down and either find an answer or ask someone to find an answer later or consult with a knowledgeable person after the session.

- Consider involving group members in various aspects of the group session, such as asking for volunteers to read scripture, to read the closing prayer or say their own, and so forth.

- Before each group session, pray for God's presence, guidance, and power; and pray throughout the study. Pray weekly or daily for your group members by name and for what God may do in their lives. More than anything else, prayer will encourage and empower you as you lead the group.

- If you truly want your small group to be successful, make sure you contact all absentees.

- Don't forget that some people find working on a service project with the group or organizing an event for the group just a meaningful to their spiritual growth as group discussion.

- It takes a dedicated leader to make any group go well. Thank you for your commitment. Blessings on your ministry.

CPSIA information can be obtained
at www.ICGtesting.com
Printed in the USA
LVOW12s2350280717
543065LV00001B/216/P